Zicklin School of Business Financial Markets Series

Series Editor
Robert A. Schwartz
Zicklin School of Business
Baruch College - CUNY
New York, NY, USA

Zicklin School of Business Financial Markets Conference Series Baruch College, CUNY

The sequence of securities markets conferences at Baruch College's Zicklin School of Business in New York City are recorded in this popular series.

The conferences are hosted by the college for industry professionals, regulators and academicians. These books are much more than historical documents. The transcripts from the conferences were carefully edited for clarity, perspective and context. Materials were included from subsequent interviews with the panelists and speakers. Each book is focused on a well delineated topic, but all deliver broader insights into the quality and efficiency of the U.S. equity markets and the dynamic forces changing them.

Robert A. Schwartz • John Aidan Byrne
Eileen Stempel
Editors

Liquidity

How to Find it, Regulate it, Get it

Springer

Editors
Robert A. Schwartz
Zicklin School of Business
Baruch College - CUNY
New York, NY, USA

John Aidan Byrne
Rockaway, NJ, USA

Eileen Stempel
Zicklin School of Business
Baruch College - CUNY
New York, NY, USA

ISSN 2627-521X ISSN 2627-5228 (electronic)
Zicklin School of Business Financial Markets Series
ISBN 978-3-031-36913-1 ISBN 978-3-031-36914-8 (eBook)
https://doi.org/10.1007/978-3-031-36914-8

This Springer imprint is published by the registered company Springer Nature Switzerland AG
The registered company address is: Gewerbestrasse 11, 6330 Cham, Switzerland

Paper in this product is recyclable.

Preface

The title of this Conference is, "Liquidity: How to Find it, Regulate it, Get It." I could have started with how to define it!

As you know, I'm an academician. In our profession, we always start by defining things. Yet I figured a definition wouldn't fly as well for this conference. Instead, I came up with key words that reflect the theme of this conference. I wanted to get your attention.

I will control myself and not get right into what exactly liquidity is. For the first time in the history of this conference series, I have put myself, with Larry Tabb's permission, on a panel. I can speak up then.

We have an excellent program. Ranier Riess, Director General of the Federation of European Securities Exchanges, came all the way across the Atlantic to be with us as a keynote speaker. Michael Piwowar, Commissioner of the U.S. Securities and Exchange Commission, came all the way from Washington, DC. Michael, as a keynote speaker, will have a very thought-provoking dialog with Larry Tabb.

I thank Larry Tabb for his partnering with me in the organization of this conference. It has meant a lot to me working closely with Larry.

We owe a huge debt of gratitude to our sponsors: BATS Global Markets; BIDS Trading; CBOE Holdings, CODA Markets; Instinet; Modern Markets Initiative; NASDAQ; OTC Markets Group, Inc.; Portware, a Factset Company; and, of course, The TABB Group.

The proceedings of this conference will be transcribed for another book in our Zicklin School of Business Financial Markets Conference Series. These books, published by Springer, are widely read. We have had a huge number of chapter downloads by thousands of readers. Our publisher, Springer, is pleased as, of course, are we.

The popularity of our conference content extends to other publications. For example, Andy Brooks' Baruch conference panel discussion was published in the

Journal of Trading, Winter 2014.[1] In response to that panel discussion, Ian Domowitz wrote a critical commentary, published by the *Journal of Trading*, that set off a lively debate. Ian and I are still friends even though he offered a sharp critique that I, with total right on my side, disagreed with. Meanwhile, a couple of years ago, co-editor John Byrne and I were reviewing a keynote address by Richard Lindsey, a principal at Callcott Group LLC, from his perspective as the landmark regulation's chief architect.[2] Lindsey had been Director of Market Regulation at the Securities and Exchange Commission when the regulation was enacted. We both agreed that Lindsey's analysis was fascinating and informative, and that it deserved wider visibility. So, John and I teamed up with Rich and turned his Baruch presentation into "The SEC's Order Handling Rules of 1997 and Beyond," a paper published by the *Journal of Portfolio Management*, Spring 2016.[3]

I have one more publishing success to tell you about. Tim Mahoney, Nazli Sila Alan, and I, motivated by an exchange we had during an earlier conference, put our heads together and produced "Combatting Turbulence in the Equity Market: Get the Listed Companies On Board." The paper was published as an invited editorial in the *Journal of Portfolio Management*, Summer, 2015.[4] Let's continue today with more excellent content on market structure.

New York, NY, USA Robert A. Schwartz

[1] What Makes an Exchange a Unique Institution? Robert A. Schwartz and John Aidan Byrne. *Journal of Trading, Institutional Investor.* Winter 2014. Vol 9. No 1: pp 22–23.

[2] Baruch College's Financial Markets Conference, "Rapidly Changing Securities Markets: Who are the Initiators?" October 23, 2012.

[3] The SEC's Order Handling Rules of 1997 and Beyond: *Perspective and Outcomes of the Landmark Regulation* Richard Lindsey, John Aidan Byrne and Robert A. Schwartz The Journal of Portfolio Management Spring 2016, 42 (3) 56–64; DOI: https://doi.org/10.3905/jpm.2016.42.3.056

[4] INVITED EDITORIAL.

Combating Turbulence in the Equity Market: *Get the Listed Companies on Board.* Nazli Sila Alan, Timothy Mahoney and Robert A. Schwartz. The Journal of Portfolio Management Summer 2015, 41 (4) 8–11; DOI: https://doi.org/10.3905/jpm.2015.41.4.008

List of Participants

Name	Company	Title
Robert Barnes	Turquoise, LSEG	CEO
Ayan Bhattacharya	Zicklin School of Business, Baruch College	Professor of Finance
Bryan Christian	Bats Global Markets	Senior Vice President, Head of U.S. Sales
R. Cromwell Coulson	OTC Markets Group, Inc.	President, CEO & Director
Ian Domowitz	ITG Solutions Network	Managing Director, CEO
Will Dove	Chief Executive Officer	Extraordinary Re
Amy Edwards	U.S. Securities and Exchange Commission	Assistant Director, Office of Markets
David Firmin	Instinet	Head of Algorithmic Trading Sales, Americas
Bill Harts	Money Markets Initiative	CEO
William Looney	CBOE	Director - Institutional Development
Phil Mackintosh	KCG	Head of Trading Strategy & Analysis
Tim Mahoney	BIDS	CEO
Jeffrey McCarthy	Nasdaq	Head of ETP Listings & Services
Michael Piwowar	U.S. Securities and Exchange Commission	Commissioner
Rainer Riess	Federation of European Securities Exchanges	Director General
Jim Ross	CODA Markets	Managing Director of Institutional Equities
Justin Schack	Rosenblatt Securities	Managing Director/Partner
Robert Schwartz	Zicklin School of Business, Baruch College	Speiser Professor of Finance
Larry Tabb	TABB Group	CEO

Name	Company	Title
Henry Waelbroeck	Portware, a Factset Company	Director of Research
Bruce Weber	Alfred Lerner College of Business, University of Delaware	Dean
Dave Weisberger	IHS-Markit	Managing Director, Trading Services
Greg Wojciechowski	The Bermuda Stock Exchange	President & CEO

Conference Sponsors

Bats Global Markets
BIDS Trading
CBOE Holdings, Inc.
CODA Markets
Instinet
Modern Markets Initiative
Nasdaq
OTC Markets Group, Inc.
Portware, *a Factset Company*
TABB Group

Contents

Chapter 1
Indexing, ETFs and Robos: Are Stocks an Endangered Species?

Robert A. Schwartz, Larry Tabb, Ayan Bhattacharya, William Looney, Jeff McCarthy, and Phil Mackintosh

LARRY TABB: I am delighted to moderate this panel on indexing, ETFs, and robos. Are single stocks an endangered species? That's our theme. Let me start by noting the shift from active to passive trading over the last couple of years. That will also be our focus as we look at single stocks.

The role of passive investing has accelerated in the last few years. In sum, there's approximately $2.2 or $3 trillion worth of ETFs; another trillion or so of passive investing, or passive-type strategies. For years, we've been seeing the random walk theory kind of play out in this market. Hey, look, you know, it's hard to consistently pick winning stocks, and so the hell with it. I'll just go pick an index! That's the current mindset. More and more, folks are increasingly doing that.

R. A. Schwartz (✉) · A. Bhattacharya
Zicklin School of Business, Baruch College - CUNY, New York, NY, USA
e-mail: robert.schwartz@baruch.cuny.edu

L. Tabb
CEO, Tabb Group, New York, NY, USA

W. Looney
CBOE, New York, NY, USA

J. McCarthy
NASDAQ, New York, NY, USA

P. Mackintosh
KCG, New York, NY, USA

R. A. Schwartz et al. (eds.), *Liquidity*, Zicklin School of Business Financial Markets Series, https://doi.org/10.1007/978-3-031-36914-8_1

Let me open with Phil. Is the single stock an endangered species, or are stock pickers dead? Will passive investing, therefore, take over the world?[1]

PHIL MACKINTOSH: I definitely don't think stock picking is dead, or that indexing will take over the world. One of the really interesting developments from my perspective is just how ETFs have started to grow as part of the index story. But when you look at the ETFs, a lot of the trading is macro-driven hedge funds, buying different factors, different sectors, different countries. That, by definition, is actually doing stock selection on a portfolio basis. So there's definitely a lot of stock selection on a portfolio basis because of the way that ETFs are letting investors get into the market.

Another thing that will drive it going forward is the new DOL fiduciary rule.[2] That will focus a lot of investment advisors on making sure that they're allocating assets for their investors in a cost-effective way. I believe index funds will benefit from that. But the good stock pickers will still be able to attract assets.

TABB: Jeff, you are seeing a dramatic shift in your business at the exchange. How do you look at it?

JEFF MCCARTHY: I agree with everything Phil said on the trends. A lot of the things supporting the movement into passive products versus active products has also been fees and performance. Phil talked about the nature of, or touched on, the products, so there are products that touch every asset class. People are kind of active in stock picking, via an ETF, into different sectors and asset classes.[3]

But you have the phenomenon of fee pressure, as well, and performance. ETFs on average have an expense ratio of 25 basis points in the US across products. That is a lot less expensive product than others, which investors are gravitating towards. I read a report measuring their performance over the last 10 years, showing that 83 percent of active fund managers did not beat their benchmarks. When you couple that with the lower fees and the selection of ETFs, being able to get asset class exposure, you are seeing a drive into these products.

TABB: Bill, isn't this only just happening on the single stock side? Are you seeing a shift in your single stock business versus the ETF business?

---

[1] Passive investing is a long-term strategy in which investors buy and hold a diversified mix of assets in an effort to match, not beat, the market. The most common passive investing approach is to buy an index fund whose holdings mirror a particular or representative segment of the financial market. Passive investing is the opposite of active investing, a more vigorous strategy offering bigger short-term gains but greater risk and volatility. Source: businessinsider.com

[2] DOL Fiduciary Rule: What Employers Should Know | NPPG-FS www.nppg.com/news/fiduciary-rule/

Everything You Need to Know About the DOL Fiduciary Rule https://www.investopedia.com/updates/dol-fiduciary-rule/updates/dol-fiduciary-rule/

Source: Katelyn Peters. Investopedia.

Updated July 14, 2021.

[3] Historically, index investing was thought of as a passive activity, i.e., you're just "buying the market." But over time, people have come to use index-based products like ETFs as proxies for different subsectors of the market (for example, Select Sector SPDRs), and then actively traded those subsector products.

WILLIAM LOONEY: Absolutely. The index option business year over year is up 3 percent versus the multi-list business, which itself encompasses both ETFs and single stocks, and is down 3 percent year over year.[4] If we want to dig a little deeper, 30 percent of our volume on the CBOE is traded in equities, 26 percent is ETFs, and 41 percent is index business.

Certainly, from the CBOE's perspective, the index options business will dominate because of our various licensing agreements with the index providers. But if you look at the options business overall from a national volume level year to date, 49 percent comprises equities, 41 percent is ETF, and 10 percent is index. As I look at those numbers over the past 3–5 years, ETFs are slowly creeping up and becoming much more of a part of the options market.

Another interesting statistic is the growth in option-based mutual funds, closed-end funds, and ETFs. In December 2000, we had 10 funds that traded options, 56 in December 2008, and then over 120 in December 2015. You can see the growth of these various options-based mutual funds and ETF structures.

The last point I'll make is, specific to the options side, the market breadth. These numbers are somewhat dated, coming from a conference I attended back in January of this year. I didn't have a chance to update them. But if you go back 5 years, over 35 names created roughly 50 percent of the average daily volume in the overall options business, so there was significant market breadth on the options side. Now we have 15 names, and almost half of those 15 are ETFs. In other words, today only 15 names dominate the landscape of liquidity. There has been a significant tightening of liquidity in the marketplace today because it is now hyper-focused on a handful of names, as opposed to years past when the market was much broader.

TABB: I guess it's not bad news, but it's certainly news that shifts the way we think about the markets in the world. Phil, is this a cost thing, or is this just an economic thing? Is this equilibrium quantity (QE) or just cost structure?[5] You guys have a very significant market making unit on both sides. How do you look at this versus just the way that it is?

MACKINTOSH: It's an asset allocation question. I think a lot of people have done Core Plus types of investment.[6] This is interesting to us. For example, seeing how the equity market structure (which ETFs are a part of) solves the trading cost problem better in this asset class (equities) than in a lot of the other asset classes we have been looking at (as in how bond ETFs trade versus how bond markets trade). There has been a lot of discussion recently about bond market structure and bond transparency. But bond trading is still really manual, and the actual trades don't show up, the treasuries don't show up on any tape anywhere. For example, the HYG

---

[4] The multi-list business refers to single stocks and ETFs trading across multiple exchanges.

[5] The speaker refers to QE, as in the economic term for equilibrium quantity, not quantitative easing.

[6] Phil Macintosh is talking about so-called "Core Plus" funds, where managers start with a core base of investments, often implemented by owning ETFs, but then are allowed to add to (think "Plus") that core with single stock investments that they might consider attractive.

or JNK ETFs and a lot of the other ETFs are the price discovery vehicles now.[7] Because they trade with 1 cent spreads, which is just basis points wide, it's much easier for asset allocators to use the ETF to get in and out of the asset classes, rather than to buy the physical, and then have to unwind the physical position.

Therefore, costs, even from the trading costs perspective, are definitely driving some of this trend.

TABB: On the bond side, are you looking at the ETFs almost like we used to look at Chicago leading New York, with futures kind of leading the cash side in the trading markets in both cities? Are we starting to see the ETFs leading the bonds?

MACKINTOSH: The amount of liquidity that's in the bond ETFs is still less than is seen in the underlying markets. From memory, the high-yield bonds and the corporate bonds trade about $3 billion a day; the underlying trade about $20 billion a day, so that's still just a fraction in the overall marketplace. One of the problems with bonds is that there is no transparency on the trading, and there are no prints of the trades. The indexes, themselves, are often really stale calculations.

Today, the HYG ETF is actually starting to trade at a discount to the index.[8] To your point, Larry, it's showing price discovery because HYG is trading cheaper than the index. But the reality is that the index is actually slow. What you're seeing is a more current price coming out of these ETFs that people are making bids and offers in than is probably coming out of the broader market.

TABB: Ayan, how do you guys see it from an academic standpoint? How do you see this balance between active and passive, and ETFs versus single stocks?

AYAN BHATTACHARYA: Let me take a step back as to how academics first started thinking about it. Why we have investment, indexes, and these passive funds and so on has been a big mystery for academics. Suppose, for example, costs were eliminated or were not present. In a frictionless world, why should you have these so-called redundant assets?[9]

In this regard, there were a number of influential papers in the 1990s and 2000s. The consensus that emerged in academia was that you have what's called a

[7] Prior to 2002, there was no market data for bonds, until NASD/FINRA established the TRACE ticker tape. According to some critics, there are many loopholes for what must be reported. Some transactions don't have to be reported at all, like treasuries. Macintosh is asserting that the data on TRACE is not, in effect, a "true" indication of bond prices. In other words, he contends the prices paid for bonds that are actually purchased by ETF managers are a much better indication of the correct price. HYG ETF is the iShares iBoxx High Yield Corporate Bond Fund; JNK ETF is the State Street SPDR Barclays Capital High Yield Bond.

[8] The bond index used by the HYG ETF is the Markit iBoxx USD Liquid High Yield Index, which presumably sources bond price data from TRACE and other places, but as discussed above, this data may be inaccurate. Mackintosh calls it "slow." Therefore, as one analyst explains, "smart investors" are willing to pay more or less for the ETF when they believe there is a mispricing in the index.

[9] Redundant assets are those assets that are not specifically required by a company to generate earnings and cash flow from operations. They are "redundant" to the operations of the business. Source: Divestopedia.

separating equilibrium in the active/passive markets.[10] That means that the risk-taking informed traders would prefer the active assets because it involves making a model of the world, figuring out where the correlations are going and so on. There is risk involved, and there is information gathering involved.

So risk-taking informed traders go into the active assets while passive assets are mostly risk averse, involving traders who are less informed, who have exogenous reasons to trade. That's the separation that academia thinks about when we look at these two asset classes.

If you accept that model, trying to understand why there has been this huge growth in passive markets, which we started out with, academia says there could be two big reasons. One is demographics. In the developed world, the population is aging, so consequently people overall are getting more risk averse. That's one reason why there is probably more investment in the passive assets. The second reason academicians give is that there has been a huge decline in the risk appetite after the financial crisis of 2008.

If one accepts that these are the two main reasons why there has been this huge increase in interest in the passive side of the market, then going down the line, the demographics are not going to change, so that part stays constant. It's the other part which is the risk appetite going down after 2008, where we might see a moderation as time goes on. But it will be interesting to see how things continue from here.

TABB: Jeff, right now, is about a quarter or so of the market kind of passive? Is there an end tipping point here? Certainly, the growth is more toward the passive side. Do we think there can be a natural balance somewhere?

McCarthy: I do think that passive assets will continue to grow. I also think that there will be an ecosystem where passive and active strategies do exist side by side and will be used. The markets are a cyclical phenomenon. So, yes, if you look at stock funds today, indexing only represents about 20 percent of the assets. There still are large pools within the active management.

I would note an S&P study which showed that over one 10-year period, 82 percent of large investment stock pickers did not outperform their benchmarks. At the same time, I also think that active strategies sometimes do outperform in other types of markets, in down markets, or in volatile markets. In down markets, active managers have more flexibility to take cash and do more cash equitization or hold more cash to help with the performance.

Active funds still have large marketing behind them.[11] If you have a cycle where you have 1 or 2 years of a portfolio manager beating the benchmark, that is often advertised, it's often marketed, and then you will see inflows into those active products at that period of time. I do think that you will consistently see a kind of ebb and flow and balance in between active and passive, but passive has a lot of room to grow.

[10] For more, see Game Theory. Muhamet Yildiz http://web.mit.edu/14.12/www/02F_slides_sig.pdf

[11] Jeff McCarthy is referring to how companies spend money on marketing their funds. Critics note how brokers and advisors sell fund products to their clients and receive 12b-1 fees in return. ETFS are not allowed to pay these fees.

Another phenomenon is that, when you look at this overall debate, there are, in fact, two separate debates. There is a debate about passive versus active, and then there's a debate that sometimes gets mixed into this, of the mutual fund versus an ETF. And a lot of ETFs, partly because of regulation over the years, did indexing and became kind of a quasi-active business where there were a lot of indexed providers. They came out with a lot of methodologies that were not traditional index methodologies. They really tried to achieve more of an alpha in an index, especially with the ETF market because it made launching that product easier with the regulators. That's because of how the SEC saw the passive versus active product.

TABB: Phil, how do you think this goes? Do we wind up crowding out the active guys? Is this just a cheap beta play?

MACKINTOSH: There are other academic studies out there even now that I've read that say that there is alpha for a stock picker.[12] It's just that it's not enough on average to overweigh the fees that the mutual funds are being charged. We're potentially going to see a little bit of economies of scale and cost compression come through the active side of the industry, which will help them deliver alpha in the long term.

I was at a conference last week talking about MiFID.[13] MiFID is really going to force the European asset managers to look at their cost structures a lot and potentially strip some of the costs out of managing money. Now maybe that is a good thing to help them get more alpha out of their portfolio.

There is definitely alpha in stock picking. But we need to get to an economies of scale level where the fees that get charged come down below the level of alpha.

TABB: To your point, we're starting to see some consolidation in the active management space. We saw Janus and a couple of other guys announce mergers, so that seems to be happening.

In terms of this push toward passive, Ayan, you had talked a little bit about how it is almost kind of a step back to say, "Hey, look, I don't know where the market is going. I'm just going to take a macro play, and I'm just going to be a little bit more passive on the market!" But institutions are starting to embrace ETFs, as well, right?

BHATTACHARYA: There is this big movement toward ETFs. If you have this huge flow into ETFs and passive assets, the question is what percentage of the market stays active, and what percentage of the market do we still want to stay active? We would tell you that without active players in the market, you wouldn't have good

[12] Mackintosh is speaking from the standpoint of an efficient market theory adherent. The common wisdom for them is that you can't beat the index, ergo there should be zero alpha, or outperformance. But there have been some (hotly debated) studies that say active managers ("stock pickers") can, in fact, choose stocks that outperform and thus generate alpha. But he goes on to say that even if these managers can do better, the amount they do better by is less than what they charge the funds. So in effect, the end investor does not benefit from it.

[13] Markets In Financial Instruments Directive. What is MiFID II and how will it affect EU's financial industry? Far-reaching rules will have a big impact on everything from banks to brokers. *Financial Times*. September 15, 2017 https://www.ft.com/content/ae935520-96ff-11e7-b83c-9588e51488a0

price discovery. That's because someone has to figure out how to put the information into the prices.[14]

Where is the tipping point? The second question is, can the market self-regulate to figure out that this is where you stop, and you move from passive to active? Or do you need regulatory intervention?[15] Once again, there are a lot of academic studies. For instance, Maureen O'Hara and I have been studying ETFs. Our studies show that more price discovery in these passive assets like ETFs can result in discrepancies in markets. We're referring here to herding effects, markets moving in cycles, and so on, the basic idea being simple.[16] It's what Keynes said many decades ago, that markets can stay irrational for longer than you can stay solvent.[17] A discrepancy which should correct by itself can stay persistent if you do not have the self-correcting mechanisms or if you don't have the right kind of market structure.[18]

The big question really is whether we require regulatory intervention or market structure changes; or can the market, by itself, figure out where the tipping point is?

TABB: Bill, you're on the institutional side, you see a lot of institutions. You guys even bought a company that's kind of in this space, too. Are you seeing more institutional flow on the passive side?

LOONEY: Very much so, it's a key business strategy for CBOE. CBOE firmly believes that the passive investment strategies will grow at an above average rate for the foreseeable future. Look at two elements of our strategy. One is our option-based index benchmarks.[19] In this regard, you can go back 10, 15 years and look at our covered write index.[20] Now we're venturing into our most recently launched SMILE Index. This index looks at the curve of implied volatility and is based on that measurement, either instructing investors to sell strangles versus their S&P 500 portfolio or to sell risk reversals, depending upon the level of puts versus calls that are being purchased.[21]

---

[14] This refers to the idea that the dynamics of trading itself allows information to enter prices in the discovery process.

[15] By self-regulate, Bhattacharya is referring to finding the equilibrium endogenously.

[16] Herding in financial markets refers to a situation whereby a group of investors intentionally adopt the actions of other investors by trading in the same direction over a period of time.

[17] John Maynard Keynes—Background and Career, Notable Works, Legacy corporatefinanceinstitute.com/resources/knowledge/economics/john-maynard-keynes/

[18] Self-correcting mechanism refers to endogenous equilibrium.

[19] Cboe US Indices https://www.cboe.com/us/indices/indicessearch/
Source: CBOE.

[20] Ibid.

[21] The CBOE Smile Index ("SMILE Index" or "Index") is a benchmark that measures the performance of a hypothetical option strategy. The strategy overlays a combination of S&P 500 25 delta put and call options (SPX options) on an investment in 1-month Treasury Bills. The T-Bills collateralize the options. The objective is to capture the volatility premium embedded in SPX options but to mitigate the risk of a short call exposure should the S&P 500 increase. The strategy relies on the ratio of put and call prices to gauge that risk. The put position is always short, but the call position switches from short to long when the put/call price ratio falls below a specified threshold. Investors often encapsulate the curve of implied volatilities at a given maturity by the ratio of

Now we have CBOE Vest, in which we have a majority ownership.[22] CBOE Vest is an option-based mutual fund company, which just published its S&P Buffer Protect Index.[23] It is a defined benefit distribution product.

In terms of the pension funds, and some of the mutual funds that we see getting involved in making commitments to these types of strategies I just spoke about, I can add this: It's very large and it's very robust.

TABB: It's not just individuals like me saying I can't pick Coke or Pepsi. I'll just take an index instead of a single stock name. It's really a whole broad spectrum of market participants.

LOONEY: I don't want to go too much off on a tangent, but to Ayan's remarks regarding regulatory intervention, perhaps we need less of it. I'll be the lone guy. The reality is that a lot of the macro factors, such as the geopolitical factors and central bank involvement around the globe since the financial crisis, are causing a lot of managers to shy away from stock picking.[24] I'll take a little bit of a leap and throw it out there. I think that's a big factor that has contributed to some of these passive-type investment strategies.

TABB: Jeff, we are starting to see liquidity. Bill talked a little bit about Smile curves and volume curves and things like that. But we're starting to see something new. In the past, it used to be a market with high volumes in the morning; high volumes toward the close and then volume would go lower in the midday. Now volume at the open is starting to be a little bit less, and it seems like all the volume is happening toward the end of the day. Does that have to do with this balancing of passive investments, or is it something else? How do you see this shaping up with liquidity?

MCCARTHY: There is probably a correlation between the two. I don't know if it's a direct shift of the passive approach changing kind of the way that you see the Smile curve. I mean, we did look at 2010 through 2016 and I agree the volume spikes more toward the close than at the open, and certainly more during the

---

implied volatilities of 25 delta put and call options. The implied volatilities of SPX options form a slope that is similar to a smile, which skews during volatile periods. The shape of the smile is viewed as an indicator of future market conditions. The SMILE Index does not use contributed input data, and all of the input data is readily available via public sources. The SMILE Index is nonsignificant, as defined by EU Regulation 2016/1011 ("EU Benchmark Regulation" or "EU BMR"). Source: CBOE.

[22] CBOE Vest is a majority-owned subsidiary of CBOE Holdings, Inc. (NASDAQ: CBOE), the holding company of the Chicago Board Options Exchange (CBOE), which is the largest US options exchange and creator of listed options.

[23] S&P Buffer Protect Index https://www.indexologyblog.com/2019/01/07/defensive-buffer-protect-option-strategies-can-help-investors-stay-the-course/

Source: S&P Dow Jones Indices.

[24] Referring to actions by Central Bank to drive interest rates to near zero, triggering a flood of "cheap money" and a stock market frenzy by investors that motivates money managers to stay away from individual stock picking in a rising stock market. "How can a money manager beat that kind of market? He can't," said Looney in a follow-up. "The manager is going to try to run with the market by buying into the S&P 500, for instance, with investors buying/selling options against them to try to generate additional yield in an effort to outperform the benchmark's return."

continuous. But we observed, at least through our economic research, that that's pretty much been the consistent trend from 2010 to 2016 with some variations.

So you do see more of a spike at the close, and that is correlated with passive investments, especially ETFs. Because there is a desire to get close to the net asset value of that ETF. That is more likely going to happen at the close, and in the closing price of that product. When you look at the underlying components of the ETFs, and the liquidity within those, how are those components traded? They're either delivered in kind—as everyone knows from the ETF mechanism—but also in order to either buy those baskets or obtain those baskets to hedge, or to deliver through that primary market mechanism, there is someone who needs to buy or sell those securities in some instances, too. You see a lot of that activity trying to match up around the close. That's really related to the net asset value and other factors related to the close.

TABB: Phil, is that how you see it, too?

MACKINTOSH: I think that index funds are getting overly blamed for this trend. I say that because they're passive investments, like they don't trade, in other words. We can't have this argument both ways. We can't say that index funds are taking all the liquidity out of the market, and then say that they are causing closed liquidity. If you're managing an index fund, then you have cash flows you have to trade, but you don't buy and sell stocks every day. You more or less just hold them all the time.

When you think about the closing volume, we see about $10 billion a day in the options at the close, and you see a lot more than that in the sort of half hour leading up to the close. The average ETF creations and redemptions, which we said already are all over different asset classes, are probably close to $3 billion.[25] So there are not even that many creations. The creation itself is a booking transaction. It's not a market on close transaction. The ETFs, themselves, all these creations and redemptions, don't do that much trading.[26] I think it's much more the algo trading that is in the market. The fact that it's a risk control metric for anyone that's got a cash flow—whether it's an active investor or not, whether it's hedging against some sort of options game—the close is your strike price on so many of those trades. Once people start to use the close, then algorithms will put more volume against that because that's what the curve is doing. That makes more volume go in against it, and it's sort of a little bit self-fulfilling.

TABB: That's sort of the self-fulfilling prophecy.

MCCARTHY: I think that when we look at ETFs, in particular, and when products trade throughout the day, it's important to know that there are ETFs that are

---

[25] ETF creations involve a financial company, known as a sponsor, which buys a basket of stocks that represent the holdings of the ETF. These shares are put into a trust, and the sponsor issues ETF shares that represent the value of the portfolio of these holdings.

[26] Mackintosh is contending that index funds are not the cause of volatility or activity at the close because they tend to buy and hold. He also points out that ETF "creations" and "redemptions" are the transactions by which a manager or trader tenders his stocks for ETF shares (creation) or receives stock for his ETF shares. Either way, these transactions do not affect the liquidity for the stocks or the ETFs, Mackintosh notes.

really based on an institutional market, and then there are ETF strategies that I would classify as more of a retail market. You do see more of those retail market ETFs trading throughout the day. I do know some ETF sponsors who promote or suggest that investors buy into those ETFs throughout the day, versus avoiding the opening or the close.

Those institutional ETFs really drive that volume that you see, especially at the close, and if you look at the ETFs, there are, out of 1,900 ETFs, 20 ETFs account for 66 percent of the trading volume in ETFs in the US market.

TABB: It's a really limited number of high volume.

MCCARTHY: It is. And then if you look at that 20 being 66 percent. One ETF, the SPDR, represents 32 percent of that 66 percent.[27] And so it is heavily skewed to those institutional based products.

TABB: Ayan, how far do you think this can go? Do you think that this is a quarter of the market, or 25 percent of the market being passive can go to 30 percent? Can it go to 50 percent? Can it go to 70 percent? At what point in time does the tail wag the dog?

BHATTACHARYA: It's hard to put a number on it. But what we do know is that you require a certain critical number of active investors in the market for price discovery; otherwise, you are going to have price dislocations. One way to think about this question is for the entire market, per se, or the entire index, per se. We are still far away from the threshold at which price discovery issues will start arising. Passive investment strategies are still 25–30 percent of the total investment universe, not even there I guess. But there are certain assets, underlying assets, which are hard to trade wherein you have much less trading in the underlying assets, and more trading in the ETFs, or the indexes. There are ETFs on junk bonds; there's an ETF on the Greek market; and there was a period in August, 2015, at the height of the Greek bailout crisis, when the underlying markets were closed, and the ETF kept trading. And how did the ETF figure out what prices to trade at? That means that there was price discovery happening in the ETF, itself.

You have these assets where, specific small assets, wherein there is less trading in the underlying and more trading in the passive instruments. And many of these ETFs are showing signs of price dislocation. There is not much correlation in the ETF price and underlying prices, there is herding, and so on. The big question really is would this trend continue onto the entire large-scale markets as more and more markets become passive? The jury is still out. Academics would tell you that, yes, it would become a primarily passively traded markets, but let's see how it plays out.

TABB: Phil, your thoughts?

MACKINTOSH: I just think there's not many ETFs that even get close in terms of the value that they trade to the underlying value of the trades. Even SPY, which

[27] See State Street Global Advisors SPDR
https://www.ssga.com/us/en/institutional/etfs

trade $25 billion a day, is a quarter of what trades in the S&P 500 companies that are in that basket.[28]

It's a little bit like there may be herding effects in nonmarket cap-weighted indexes where there's some overweights to relatively small cap stocks. But even then, you've got to have inflows to make those stocks trade. The ETF, itself, is very good if you look across the whole spectrum at tracking NAV throughout the day.[29] I think the ETFs don't cause as much stock dislocation as people think.

I look at IWM, the small cap ETF. It trades about $4 billion to $5 billion a day. The underlying trade is about $15 billion a day.[30] So already the ETF is less liquid. But actually, the ETF is trading with a 1 cent spread or about a 1 or 2 basis point spread. The underlying would trade at the equivalent of a 25-cent spread, or a 20, 30 basis point spread. The ETF is usually so much cheaper on the bid and the offer than the actual underlying stocks that you talk about to the market makers that we have. They don't actually do stock arbitrage. Because with the ETF, you can hit the bid, you can hit the offer, and trade that full billion-dollar worth of IWM and never, ever trigger stock arbitrage.

TABB: That then leads me to think I'm much better off just trading the ETF, and the volume of ETFs and passives will wind up increasing, and the singles will decline?

MACKINTOSH: The individual who likes beta is probably pretty well placed to trade their retail investments in ETFs.[31] Because we do a lot of facilitation and wholesaling of the ETF market. It's really interesting about a third of all of the retail trading at the moment is in ETFs. If you add up that trading, they've been net buying the ETFs for the last 6 or 7 years. It adds up to about a third of the creations in ETFs. The retail investors definitely think the same way as you. It's like once they have decided that they want a beta exposure that's low cost, the ETF is a super easy vehicle to get access to a basis point or less spread.

---

[28] State Street Global Advisors Marks 25th Anniversary of the SPDR® S&P 500® ETF. World's Largest ETF Maintains Daily Trading Volume of Nearly $25 Billion.

State Street Global Advisors, the asset management business of State Street Corporation (NYSE: STT), today marked the 25th anniversary of the first ever US-listed exchange traded fund (ETF), the SPDR S&P 500 ETF (Symbol: SPY). Launched on January 29, 1993, with $6.5 million in assets, SPY is currently the world's largest ETF with more than $302 billion[1] in assets and the most traded security in the world with an average daily trading volume of $25 billion. Source: State Street Global Advisors January 29, 2018.

[29] Net Asset Value.

[30] IWM ETF Report: Ratings, Analysis, Quotes, Holdings | ETF.com.

[31] Beta is a measure of a stock's volatility in relation to the overall market. By definition, the market, such as the S&P 500 Index, has a beta of 1.0, and individual stocks are ranked according to how much they deviate from the market.

A stock that swings more than the market over time has a beta above 1.0. If a stock moves less than the market, the stock's beta is less than 1.0. High-beta stocks are supposed to be riskier but provide higher return potential; low-beta stocks pose less risk but also lower returns.

Source: Investopedia.

TABB: Then that just says, in effect, the more professional, the more traditional fund manager, actually should be doing the opposite, that is taking very strategic bets on things that they think are under- or overvalued?

MACKINTOSH: I talk to institutions as part of my job. These institutions, as we would consider them, don't trade that many ETFs. The mutual fund managers who are stock pickers are still out there picking stocks. The other sort of ETF creations that are going on, some two thirds, I think, involve a lot of the macro hedge funds. It's institutional but it's hedge funds who are making decisions.[32]

BHATTACHARYA: What empirical academic research shows is that these ETFs help in price discovery, especially when the underlying assets are hard to trade. But it's tricky. ETFs are usually an entire portfolio, it's an index, so they help price discovery at the basket level. But those prices are much more correlated together in individual assets which make up that ETF. An idiosyncratic shock to one of these assets in the basket starts affecting another asset in the basket even though that idiosyncratic shock wasn't for that other asset. It's complicated. It's not clear cut.

On August 24,[33] the market opened, the market closed for an hour, there was something happening in China, and then all the ETFs froze up. We are seeing more and more of these sorts of things happening. And we don't fully understand why it's happening. But many of us in academia believe that it's a complicated question, and we need to recognize that.

MACKINTOSH: I'm going to disagree a little bit again, just because I don't think the index funds are trading that much. What has happened since 1995 through 2005 is that we had decimalization, so spreads got tighter. We had a lot of automation. We had competitive exchanges. Transaction costs came down about 20-fold. Electronic trading has taken off in that 10-year period. That has allowed people to risk transfer between, say, a slightly rich and a slight cheap tech stock so much more quickly than they would have in the past, when they had to go down to the New York Stock Exchange floor and trade it manually with a human who might back away from a quote. Now you can do a trade, and because you are only trading two basis point spreads, you can probably make a little bit of money out of that.

The correlation that we're seeing across sectors and across the generic asset classes that tend to be the same things that indexes track is probably more than the impact of electronic trading in the market doing risk transfer across those stocks.

BHATTACHARYA: Academic studies control for those things. In this regard, academicians are careful enough there. Even after you control for things, you do see the effects. It's not yet clear exactly what is happening. The way many of us would think about it is that we don't know. That's a better approach to looking at this question rather than saying that ETFs have nothing to do with it. These huge volumes are

---

[32] See How Hedge Funds Use ETFs. Sumit Roy. www.etf.com/sections/features-and-news/how-hedge-funds-use-etfs?nopaging=1

How Hedge Funds Use ETFs | ETF.com.

[33] What happened during the August 24 "flash crash." https://www.cnbc.com/2015/09/25/what-happened-during-the-aug-24-flash-crash.html

Source: CNBC.

still coming in. We're still trying to figure out what's happening. It's better to be open and see whether ETFs are causing this. Some academic studies do show that they are. The jury is still out I would think.

TABB: I'll open it up for a couple of questions.

ATTENDEE: I teach at Baruch. I was a market maker in options on the American Stock Exchange for 20 years. Is a money manager who is using ETFs to select industries, an active investor or a passive investor?

MACKINTOSH: If it's a hedge fund they're clearly active, they're doing a lot of turnover.

ATTENDEE: So it's not clear to me, this discussion of the ETFs, as being so passive. My second observation is that, when I traded options, when options were instituted on specific equities, they increased the liquidity in that equity because there were more participants. It would seem to me the same is true with ETFs, that if there are ETFs with underlying baskets of stocks, that too has to increase the liquidity in those stocks? Am I right or wrong?

BHATTACHARYA: It gets a little trickier here. There wasn't price discovery happening in the options, per se, but today at least in some ETFs, especially in hard-to-trade assets, you're seeing price discovery in the ETF. That changes things quite a lot. If it's just passive investment on the basket, options basket, that's good for the underlying markets. But in recent years, there's price discovery happening in the ETF. Because if you have price discovery in both the ETF or the basket and the underlying markets, you have learning and feedback happening between two markets.[34] That's where the dynamics can come into play.

ATTENDEE: When there were introductions on futures on US Treasury bonds, that's where the price discovery took place. But that clearly increased the liquidity of the underlying markets. I don't follow the argument of price discovery suggesting that's not adding liquidity.

TABB: Bill, you're the options guy.

LOONEY: I don't think we're talking about options anymore per se. I agree with you that the creation of the ETFs has created additional liquidity, or the stocks that comprise the ETFs in that liquidity is what creates the liquidity in ETFs and vice versa. They play off one another. I'm more on your side of the equation. I completely agree with the statements that you're making. I think that liquidity fuels itself. I'm not going to speculate on the price discovery discussion that's happening. What I can tell you is this: In the options marketplace, the amount of equities that trade as a result is enormous, and one plays off the others.

I completely agree with your argument that the liquidity component is being fueled on both sides of the equation as these products exist. I was going to reference earlier some of the pension fund money that we've seen going into these options-based indexes. The state of Hawaii and the state of South Carolina this year have committed \$1.6 billion each into option-based put writing programs. They're

[34] Learning here refers to the fundamentals and the accompanying feedback effects. Learnings are happening at two venues simultaneously, Ayan notes in a follow-up.

benchmarking themselves against the Russell, for example, and then they're going to be actively engaged in selling options. That type of flow will create equity trades as a result, right? To your point, the whole system will fuel itself.

TABB: I guess your point is that the whole passive ETF world isn't really killing the single stock. It's just adding a level of liquidity that enables the single stock player to get in and out easier.

ATTENDEE: That's what my argument was.

TABB: Right, exactly.

MATTHEW BERGERMAN [DTCC Data Products]: What is the panel's thoughts on the coming SEC rule about liquidity reporting for mutual funds and ETFs? What kind of an impact may that have?[35]

MCCARTHY: I know that initially the thought is that ETFs will be exempt from that rule because of the in-kind transfer process. An ETF does not necessarily have to sell positions, or buy or sell securities, to deliver cash to the underlying investors (versus holding securities in kind). The liquidity components, at least initially, for many of the ETFs (the traditional ETFS not the exchange-traded products, that may hold derivatives or other instruments) would be exempt [from that rule].

MACKINTOSH: And that came out last week. I think that was how it worked; the ETFs were exempt.

MCCARTHY: Yes, for traditional ETFs, that would be excluding the ETNs or commodity-based ETPs.[36]

BOB SCHWARTZ: I'm curious because I don't know the answer. What's the holding period for ETFs? How fast is turnover compared to the underlying? Faster, slower?

MACKINTOSH: It depends. Do you mean from an investor's perspective?

SCHWARTZ: You sound like an academician!

MACKINTOSH: Or the turnover, like the actual turnover per ticker?

SCHWARTZ: Yes, what's the holding period?

MACKINTOSH: It depends. The levered ETFs have very short holding periods on average, measured in days, whereas some of the smart beta products are much longer in months, maybe years. But it really depends on the kind of underlying investor and what they're being used for.

SCHWARTZ: Does that translate into active versus passive? Does it have implications if you trade?

MACKINTOSH: Index funds, especially the ones that we were talking about earlier that are heavily traded by hedge funds as hedges, have much shorter holding

[35] US SEC Proposes Liquidity Risk Management Programs, Optional "Swing Pricing," and Liquidity Reporting for Mutual Funds and Certain ETFs | HUB | K&L Gates (klgates.com).

Www.klgates.com/US-SEC-Proposes-Liquidity-Risk-Management-Programs-Optional-Swing-Pricing-and-Liquidity-Reporting-for-Mutual-Funds-and-Certain-ETFs-10-22-2015#:~:text=Require

[36] ETNs is the acronym for Exchange Traded Notes. See What Are ETNs?—Fidelity, www.fidelity.com/learning-center/investment-products/etf/types-etfs-etns. ETPs is the acronym for Exchange Traded Products.

periods. But what it reflects is they're being used as liquidity transfer vehicles for hedging, and for shorter term equitization. Something that is more attractive to a retail investor for a buy hold strategy like a smart beta low volatility fund, or high dividend fund, will probably have investors that don't need to get in and out as fast. A lot of the ETFs are quasi-derivatives these days, say the sector SPDRs, and their turnover is a lot more like futures where people are using them just to equitize and hedge[37] because it's a much cheaper entry and exit vehicle than buying the physical.

TABB: I would like to agree with that tremendously. We just finished our institutional equity trading study. Most of the institutional investors we talked to about ETFs were using them as equitization-type products. Actually, they tend to be more competition to the futures than they actually are to anything else because they can get into, instead of just getting into the broad market, the S&P 500, and trading out of it. They can get into financials, or consumer cyclicals, or other types of ETF strategies that are more aligned with their overall strategy, and they can trade out of them.

On that final note, I want to thank everybody on our panel for this far-reaching debate.

[37] See footnote 27.

Chapter 2
How Technology Is Transforming Liquidity Provision

Robert A. Schwartz, Bruce Weber, Bryan Christian, Bill Harts, Tim Mahoney, and Henri Waelbroeck

BRUCE WEBER: Our topic is titled: How technology is transforming liquidity provision. This topic covers an area relevant to the previous panel moderated by Larry Tabb on Indexing, ETFs, and robo investing. We will now step back in the investment value chain. Earlier at this conference, we heard about front-end investment instruments, the products that are developed and promoted with investors and buy-side customers in mind. On this panel, we want to look at how well the industry is supplying liquidity to enable these new offerings to perform well for investors and to be efficiently priced. There are new trading needs out there to be met. Our focus is on liquidity provision and on something near and dear to my heart, which is information technology.

Back in 1987, one of my first research projects as a young PhD student at the University of Pennsylvania's Wharton School was to study the changes that occurred when the Big Bang deregulation hit the London financial markets, exactly 30 years

R. A. Schwartz (✉)
Zicklin School of Business, Baruch College - CUNY, New York, NY, USA
e-mail: robert.schwartz@baruch.cuny.edu

B. Weber
Alfred Lerner School of Business and Economics, University of Delaware, Newark, DE, USA

B. Christian
BATS Global Markets, New York, NY, USA

B. Harts
Modern Markets Initiative, New York, NY, USA

T. Mahoney
BIDS, New York, NY, USA

H. Waelbroeck
Portware, a Factset Company, New York, NY, USA

R. A. Schwartz et al. (eds.), *Liquidity*, Zicklin School of Business Financial Markets Series, https://doi.org/10.1007/978-3-031-36914-8_2

ago.[1] It was a great opportunity supported by a grant from AT&T, the major telecommunications provider, which realized screen-based trading and global market data transmission would also be a great opportunity for them. I was lucky enough to fly over to London with my faculty advisor, Eric Clemons, to visit the London Stock Exchange, as well as with numerous member firm dealing rooms. We gathered data and insights from senior practitioners on the earlier structure of the market, and on the impact of new IT. Many of you know that this was an initiative of the Thatcher government in the UK to deregulate and open up the financial markets in Britain. The consensus in Britain is that it was a very successful transformation. Technology was a huge part of this huge transformation, and that technology was a major part of the improvements. But we found the London Stock Exchange (LSE) also made a huge mistake leading up to the Big Bang day of October 27, 1986. The exchange had invested £3 million —US $5 million, updating and upgrading its trading floor with new technology, and member firms signed 3-year leases on trading floor space for their personnel. The traders we spoke with realized soon after, the new SEAQ display system was introduced on Big Bang day that the London trading floor, in spite of a major upgrade, was now redundant and was soon almost entirely empty.[2] The London Stock Exchange and its members had squandered millions believing that trading would still take place on the floor, even though all the LSE's quotes and price data was now displayed on electronic screens all around the world. Our trader surveys indicated that share price information was more timely on the floor before SEAQ but that traders in upstairs dealing rooms held the advantage after Big Bang. This example from 30 years ago shows that we struggle to forecast the role of technology, as it has challenged and overtaken exchange trading floors and other established practices. Our panelists today can take the long view and think about how the markets 30 years from now are going to look back in time, how participants in the market are going to respond to developments, how liquidity will be provided, and finally, at how well technology is going to be used to create better markets with more liquidity than today in 2016, 30 years after the famous Big Bang transformation.

I'll start with Bryan because you're at BATS Global Markets, which is a marketplace that facilitates automated market making and offers a significant amount of liquidity provision and trading volume. Bryan, how would you say the demand for liquidity and access to liquidity has changed in the past 10 years?

BRYAN CHRISTIAN: I'll take a mostly present-day view from a BATS perspective with respect for the past. First, we're obviously a newer exchange within this marketplace.[3] BATS wouldn't exist today if it wasn't for the changes that happened

---

[1] How the Big Bang changed the City of London forever. Jamie Robertson, Business reporter, BBC News. 26 October 2016 https://www.bbc.com/news/business-37751599?ocid=socialflow_twitter&

[2] SEAQ is London Stock Exchange's non-electronically executable quotation service that allows market makers to quote prices in a number of fixed interest securities. Source: London Stock Exchange.

[3] BATS Global Markets, founded in June 2005 by Dave Cummings, a computer programmer, is part of Cboe Global Markets as of writing in 2021.

from a regulatory standpoint. We're a marketplace that's driven by regulation, which ultimately has been driving technology.

You could look back to the multiple rules that have been changed over time, whether it is the Order Handling Rules, decimalization, and then Reg NMS.[4] We don't have a trading floor, we're all electronic, and ultimately, we utilize the opportunity for technology, to lower costs for the industry. That's a very important element we're talking about here. And then there's regulation as well. You know, ECNs, or Electronic Communications Systems, of course, really were the great enabler for the change that's out there, when you look at the different markets and from the legacy perspective. At BATS, we continue to look for new technology to drive that change and to be innovative, as well.

WEBER: To extend your description, is the automated market maker that participates in BATS, or any of the other electronic markets we see out there, a true liquidity provider, in the sense that we may be defining that in academic articles?

CHRISTIAN: From our perspective, you need to understand these markets today. The automated market maker is not only on BATS; it's on the floor of the New York Stock Exchange. In fact, they're practically everywhere in the marketplace. They're providing liquidity in all markets and in multiple asset classes beyond equities. I would say absolutely, yes, that market making on these systems is a major liquidity provider.

HENRI WAELBROECK: It gives me great pleasure to throw a wrench in an otherwise perfectly spinning wheel. The question really is what we mean by liquidity providing. And it's helpful to look at market microstructure in terms of the statistics of price fluctuations. We made a lot of progress in recent years in really understanding how the market works. It's known now from the work of Hardiman and Bouchaud that price is effectively a self-exciting Hawkes process with a power-law kernel Pareto exponent 1.15.[5] In plain English, that means all it takes for the markets to get excited is to look at itself. And you might wonder why it doesn't have a Facebook account yet!

That aside, the point is this: What's really happening at the microstructure level is the interaction of algorithmic strategies operating as an ecosystem. That's where each of these algorithmic strategies are constantly adapting to the products of the others, looking for opportunities to make a short-term profit. Does this really count as liquidity providing? One of the central properties of this critical Hawkes process is that it's effectively operating near the point of vanishing liquidity, which means a

[4]The SEC's Order Handling Rules of 1997 and Beyond: *Perspective and Outcomes of the Landmark Regulation* Richard Lindsey, John Aidan Byrne and Robert A. Schwartz The Journal of Portfolio Management Spring 2016, 42 (3) 56–64; DOI: https://doi.org/10.3905/jpm.2016.42.3.056

[5]Branching ratio approximation for the self-exciting Hawkes process. Stephen J. Hardiman, Jean-Philippe Bouchaud https://arxiv.org/abs/1403.5227

The Hawkes process (HP) is a mathematical model for these "self-exciting" processes, named after its creator Alan G. Hawkes. The HP is a counting process that models a sequence of "arrivals" of some type over time, for example, earthquakes, gang violence, trade orders, or bank defaults.

Source: arxiv.org

very small perturbation can cause a very large price change—that is to say, there are very few orders in the limit book, so even a relatively small market order can cause a very large price change.[6] And we observe this periodically through micro crashes. To call that liquidity provision is really a stretch of the imagination.

The next question is this: What is liquidity providing, who is really providing liquidity in this market? For that, you have to look at market participants that are in the business of trying to understand what price should be, at least in the current interest rate monitoring environment, as well as what is the fair price. There's relative pricing, absolute pricing models, and there are statistical arbitrage firms, quant funds. These are trying to figure out when these short-term dislocations caused by the market microstructure, and by the activity of automated market makers, lead to profitable trading opportunities—based on the slightly longer timeframe and view of what the fair price should be.

We've seen a migration in the role of the liquidity provider. In the old days, that perhaps used to be in the hands of a specialist who was really putting capital at risk. Today, that role has migrated to a new world of automated market making and is handled by funds with very little capital at risk. The larger capital in this new world really effectively acts as a liquidity provider and is currently in the hands of quant funds, and of institutional orders looking for "good" prices, mispricing, and where you profit from them.

WEBER: Bill, when I was starting in research markets, and you were really trading in these markets and subject to the rules of the late 1980s, it was pretty clear who was providing liquidity—NYSE specialists and NASDAQ dealers—and who was demanding it. Is there a higher level of ambiguity today about who is supplying liquidity and who is consuming it the way Henri has portrayed?

BILL HARTS: No, I don't think things have changed that much. The high-frequency trading firms of today that are making markets day in and day out are probably capitalized as much, or maybe even more, than the specialists and market makers of yesteryear.

The other thing I would point out is that when we talk about markets and where liquidity is, and where institutional clients especially can find liquidity, it's markets like BATS, NYSE, and NASDAQ where the vast majority of trading is happening. Nothing against Tim Mahoney, because BIDS is a fantastic place. I recommend that all institutions should try it.

TIM MAHONEY: Bill was a board member at one point!

HARTS: Frankly, there's a limit to how much natural liquidity that institutions will find trading with each other. That speaks to the role of electronic market makers today.

WEBER: Well, Tim, let me pass it off to you on BIDS place in liquidity provision today.

MAHONEY: I'll try to fill in a bunch of gaps. So far on this panel, we've had a description of the Big Bang in London, which is really cool because you don't get that a lot in a conversation on market structure, and we've also identified the Order Handling Rules and Reg NMS. I would argue that this is a story that is some four

[6] BIS Working Papers. https://www.bis.org/publ/work158.pdf

decades old, a story that stretches back into the 1970s. When I think about the evolution of the marketplace, I go back to the '75 Amendments.[7] That's really the turning point. Consider the period 1962 to 1972, when liquidity in that 10-year period on the New York Stock Exchange quadrupled to 16 million shares a day, a study showed. Block volume jumped from 1 percent to 18 percent. And as Dr. Robert Schwartz's book, *Equity Markets in Action,* clearly pointed out, that growth is all about the rise of the institutional investor.[8] That changes the story.

Back in 1975, the New York Stock Exchange was the center of power in the universe for liquidity provision. It was in the hands of the NYSE specialists. To pick a period in time, from the '75 Amendments to Reg ATS in 1998, we're talking about a transformation to the upstairs brokers, to the brokers really providing liquidity.[9] And a big part of that was NASDAQ. Think about it. NASDAQ was then really akin to the farm league in the markets. You had to be listed over-the-counter on NASDAQ first, if you were not a seasoned company. You couldn't otherwise launch an IPO on the New York Stock Exchange in 1984, so you had to go list it first on NASDAQ before you could get it listed on the Big Board.

Throughout the 1980s, the brokers then took power back. The brokers began trading more upstairs. By 1994, NASDAQ was bigger than the New York; it was the biggest marketplace in the world. By 1995, block trading accounted for 57 percent of the trades on the New York Stock Exchange. All this stuff leads to the same point; upstairs brokers were facilitating liquidity; it was no longer the specialist. It was the upstairs broker who was the primary focus of that. There was only one definition of liquidity, there was only one market, and it was in the hands of upstairs brokers.

A series of interesting things happened: It's an intersection of regulation and technology. For me, the big one was the Crash of 1987.[10] As we came out of the

[7] Federal legislation launched on June 4, 1975, to amend the Securities Exchange Act of 1934. The 1975 amendments instructed the Securities and Exchange Commission to cooperate with the industry in creating a National Market System along with an ambitious system for the clearance and settlement of securities transactions nationwide. The amendments also provided for the prohibition of fixed-commission rates, promulgated earlier by the SEC in its Rule 19b-3.

[8] Equity Markets in Action: The Fundamentals of Liquidity, Market Structure & Trading. Robert A. Schwartz, Reto Francioni. August 2004, Wiley & Sons, Inc.

[9] The term "upstairs"—upstairs brokers, upstairs trading, for example—originated back in the days when the New York Stock Exchange floor was the dominant market. Trades that occurred "upstairs" were transacted away from and off the floor, that is to say "upstairs." The "upstairs" market became, in effect, the market for off-exchange block trading of a listed security, NASDAQ being a notable example. Many of these trades today are transacted within a broker-dealer firm, with the broker-dealer as the agent for both counterparties.

Reg ATS: https://www.sec.gov/rules/final/34-40760.txt

[10] Stock Market Crash of 1987. Black Monday

"The first contemporary global financial crisis unfolded in the autumn of 1987 on a day known infamously as "Black Monday." A chain reaction of market distress sent global stock exchanges plummeting in a matter of hours. In the United States, the Dow Jones Industrial Average (DJIA) dropped 22.6 percent in a single trading session, a loss that remains the largest one-day stock market decline in history. At the time, it also marked the sharpest market downturn in the United States since the Great Depression." Source: Stock Market Crash of 1987. Federal Reserve History. Donald Bernhardt and Marshall Eckblad, Federal Reserve Bank of Chicago. https://www.federalreservehistory.org/essays/stock_market_crash_of_1987

Crash, the talk then turned to SOES, NASDAQ'S Small Order Execution System.[11] Before this, we had no concept of auto execution. Because NASDAQ market makers were accused of not picking up their phones from other market participants calling about their orders, you ended up with this concept known as SOES.[12] People took advantage of SOES, such as the SOES Bandits perhaps. Others who arguably took advantage of it, in general, were well-known market figures like Jerry Putnam and Josh Levine, who became frontrunners in the development of ATSs.[13]

This concept of auto execution was transformational. It fundamentally changed the whole world. In 1997, sixteenth pricing began and the buy-side, in effect, then started trading on their own.[14] And that disrupted the entire ecosystem.

Let me explain: Before 1997, commissions were at 5–7 cents a share; spreads at a quarter of a point. By 2008, we had penny spreads and commissions of 2–3 cents. That just changed the role of the broker dealer. And, consequently, the broker dealer's traditional role disappeared. At issue here was the traditional role of the liquidity provider, which is to say an upstairs broker, who basically was facilitating that with commissions. But now you have this complete disruption we're experiencing today. At the same time, these same aforementioned market participants were still being subsidized by banking fees, if you recall the implication of the related Global Analyst Research Settlement of 2003.[15] Therefore, once you had eliminated the

[11] The Small Order Execution System (SOES) is a computer network that automatically executed trades in NASDAQ market securities and some NASDAQ small cap securities. SOES enabled individual investors to execute trades in fast-moving markets and gave them the same access to orders and execution as larger traders. Source: Investopedia.

[12] The Price of Backing Away: Trading: Nasdaq market makers often don't honor the prices they display. Complaints abound, but NASD says most are frivolous. SCOT J. PALTROW, OCT. 23, 1994. *Los Angeles Times* https://www.latimes.com/archives/la-xpm-1994-10-23-fi-53742-story.html

[13] SOES Bandits: The Cowboy Day Traders of the '90s and What We Can Learn From Them. Pat Crawley. Blog. Warrior Trading. https://www.warriortrading.com/soes-bandits/#:~:text=The%20SOES%20(small%20order%20execution,the%20market%20makers'%20quoted%20price

Alternative Trading Systems (ATS). *Investopedia.* James Chen. April 18, 2019. https://www.investopedia.com/terms/a/alternative-trading-system.asp

[14] Pricing in increments of one eight stopped in 1997.

[15] SEC Fact Sheet on Global Analyst Research Settlements
https://www.sec.gov/news/speech/factsheet.htm

2003 Global Settlement. FINRA. https://www.finra.org/rules-guidance/guidance/reports/2003-global-settlement

"In addition to fines and disgorgement," according to a summary of key aspects of the Settlement in a detail story, "all 12 firms involved in the settlement agreed to significantly alter the way they do business, including formally separating their research and investment banking departments."

Added this summary: "No longer are the firms allowed to engage in a practice common during the stock market bubble of the late 1990s: dangling the promise of glowing research coverage in front of companies the banks hoped to help bring public through initial stock offerings. The 12 firms also agreed to curtail the practice of doling out coveted initial public offering shares to favored clients."

Source: Ben White, Research Settlement Completed.
Washington Post. August 27, 2004.

ability to subsidize the banking fees, you took away the excess commissions. As a result, you have this lack of liquidity providers.

And that really is what you have today. It is a tale of two markets. If you're trading 100 shares, it's the best market you've ever seen in your life. There is more of this 100-share liquidity than you could ever imagine. The traditional market maker has been replaced by the automated market maker in one way or another, and spreads are tighter. But if you're trading 100,000 shares, if you're an institutional investor, it's very difficult. If you interview market participants, that's what you will find. For the traditional, fundamental investor, this market is the worst in the world. It doesn't work. Yet if you talk to the retail investor, it's the absolute best market. It's cheap and easy to trade. Passive investors can trade.

This tale of two markets is a result of the evolution of this marketplace. We're still in the process of trying to solve this challenge for the traditional institutional investor. Places like ours—thanks for the plug, Bill!—are really helpful. But there is a lot of work still to be done.

HARTS: Hold on a second. Wait a minute. We hear this from a lot of institutions. Oh, it's really hard for us to trade now because markets are more fragmented, and there are smaller pieces of liquidity around. But everything we see points to the fact that institutions are now embracing technology that enables them to trade better in these markets. It seems like every day I read about another big buy-side firm that's routing directly to a high-frequency trading firm or is using HFT technology, HFT smart routers, or other services. I mean, maybe it's harder, in the sense that you can no longer call a large broker and ask for a block size quote. But maybe it's not so much harder if you're embracing the technology to trade in today's markets.

MAHONEY: Technology solves some of our problems, but not all of them. I do think the multiple day position has always been hard and continues to be hard. The other thing we haven't talked about is this: There's been a concentration of assets. Scale on the buy-side was mentioned today. You need scale to lower your fees. Part of the downside here is that as you get more assets concentrated among fewer and fewer market participants, those 3–5 percent positions they put on become more and more difficult to trade.

Several factors are worth noting. Even in the old market structure environment, it would have been more complicated to try and trade institutional against retail. Today, the bigger positions are being concentrated in the hands of the winning alpha providers. And the hundred-share stuff doesn't get you there fast enough. The fear is that by trying to interact with the hundred-share stuff, you just can't get the order filled in a quick-enough period of time. There was a facilitation in the past where a broker trading desk would take on big positions and facilitate it. That doesn't exist anymore. And there are some block deals and a little bit of capital being used. But the reality is, in this tale of two markets, the big provider to a natural fundamental investor's liquidity is another natural fundamental investor. And as you point out, there is not a ton of that. I mean, there's a lot of people who are on the same side of all those trades.

There's a gap, and the gaps are being filled. Markets are incredibly efficient, and they evolve at a rapid pace. This is not the end of the world. These are all solvable problems over time. And liquidity definitions are changing. You might not want to trade always on Virtu's technology but still, people are doing it because it is actually helping them.

WEBER: Henri, specifically, how do you see technology driving the markets? Does this mean addressing the point Tim is making about the one-sidedness of large investors? Maybe recent trends have unwittingly segmented our markets into a retail piece, where everything is cheap and easy today, and then an institutional world where position size and exposure means you have to trade things very differently on different platforms? Are technology and intelligent computers capable of reducing the space between these two segments and enhancing overall access to liquidity?

WAELBROECK: I want to comment first on the discussion we were just having, about looking at historical trends. Not to sound like a broken record, but there is something to be learned from looking at the statistics of prices over time. There also is a very interesting story in terms of statistical trends, historical trends. You can learn the model parameters on data from pretty much any year in the past. The high-frequency cutoff, basically the minimum amount of time it takes for information to propagate to excite the next node in this process, is what has changed. That is to say, the accelerating pace of high-speed trading has changed. It has declined from about 10 seconds in the 1990s to a little bit less than a millisecond today. Essentially, you can think of it just at that level, as the same kind of market we had back in the day. It's just operating a lot faster.

MAHONEY: And that goes with the crashes, say the 1929 crash. It took 24 years after that crash to make a new high. And take the 1987 crash. It took 2 years after that to get back to where we were.

WAELBROECK: Similar story.

MAHONEY: We all talk about the Flash Crash.[16] And, quite frankly, it was soon probably 90 percent of the way back to where it started on that day of the crash. In 15 minutes, it was back to where it was. The breaks you have now, well it's over before you even know it happened.

WAELBROECK: Change is also significant in the development of machine learning techniques, which really started with statistical arbitrage back in the day. That was basically the beginning of machine learning in trading. It has led to a substantial amount of capital allocation to strategies in terms of short-term price list allocations and for opportunities to trade on mean reversion. These are the predominant liquidity providers of the day. There is a solid trend, that we're clearly part of, to use those techniques of statistical arbitrage and make them available to help institutional orders essentially benefit from the same kind of statistical footprints to optimize their execution. In doing so, the institutional orders themselves become liquidity providers as well. If it becomes more intelligent, it becomes better able to trade faster when prices are more attractive and so on.

[16] The Flash Crash of May 6, 2010 lasted about 36 minutes, erasing 998.5 points, or about 9% in the Dow Jones Industrial Average, and then quickly recouping the losses as the various indexes rapidly rebounded in this high-speed, electronic trading phenomena. At the time, it was a record one-day point decline on an intraday basis in the history of Dow Jones Industrial Average.

There's a trend there too that is creating new liquidity pools and bringing them to the table. It is being driven by the development of machine learning.

MAHONEY: And you've got to change the PM's perspective in this regard. If you deal with fundamental portfolio managers, they have to recognize that reality. Portfolio managers have to change their expectations. For instance, a buy-side manager can't give you an order to buy a mid-cap company's shares and say, "Give it to Salomon, right, and call Bill Harts up and he'll take care of it." That doesn't happen now because you have to be thoughtful, being potentially a provider where you will pick up performance. The ability to measure and capture that, and then report it back, and then the behavioral changes in the fundamental portfolio manager, do not happen in milliseconds, microseconds, days, weeks, or months. It's a longer-term change of behavior.

WAELBROECK: That's an excellent point. For that to become fully developed—and that's sort of the next frontier in machine learning—the issue is improvement of what I think of as intelligent human-machine interfaces. That is a user interface that enables the human trader or portfolio manager to be alerted to dislocations or to significant events. This is where human thought can actually complement and supplement machine intelligence to make the better decision, in terms of strategic liquidity providers.

MAHONEY: That's transaction cost analysis (TCA).[17] If you're not measuring, if you can't capture the advantage of providing liquidity, nobody will do it. It's your ability to capture that data, and to report it back in a usable format, where the end investor who's making a multiyear decision can look and say, "Wow, you know what, that was pretty good. I know I wanted to do this trade all at one time. But I did it over a week, and I actually picked up 7 basis points in relative performance to my benchmark by being patient." Therefore, it's the interface and front-end display that in a meaningful way shows the benefits and the education process that goes with that.

WEBER: Let's agree for a moment we've made access to the markets more democratic, and we've given more people entrée into liquidity provision. You used to need a special license to be a liquidity provider.[18] Now, as Henri was saying, an institutional player who's patient actually could be seen as supplying liquidity, capitalizing on mean reversion, or being a short-term contrarian. But at the same time, is that making our markets more brittle and fragile? In the sense that—by not registering that liquidity provider and by having free entry in and out of providing quotes and supporting a liquid market, you are not always making a two-way market—we've created the environment for more of these fractures and price breaks?

Bryan, I believe the average trade size in BATS is quite small. Do you see BATS playing a role in reducing the fragility that the public is observing in our markets today?

---

[17] Transaction cost analysis (TCA) is used by institutional investors to study the costs of trades in terms of the most favorable prices for the investor from purchase to sale. The analysis can be divided into pre-trade and post-trade analysis.

[18] Referring to the market structure of the recent past when regulators authorized certain groups of market participations, such as upstairs brokers, to provide liquidity via a "registration" process.

CHRISTIAN: We as a marketplace identify multiple gaps when it comes to trading and access to liquidity. Technology is the enabler for market participants to get to the pools of liquidity. We are all enablers in that sense, whether or not it is BIDS, Portware, or BATS up here. We are providing access to liquidity to other players, right? If you're a money manager sitting on a Portware front end today, you have access to multiple pools of liquidity that you never had access to before.

Yes, we have a fragmented market with multiple pools of liquidity. But we've not had this centralized sort of connectivity before and the access to these pools of liquidity within a marketplace. That has value beyond the kind of events that happen while also continuing to grow our markets from a stability standpoint. It will also help us to identify those events quicker.

To your next question, Bruce, about the market maker or the role of the market maker. The market maker, the liquidity provider within this marketplace, is very important. We ultimately have a regulated environment for a reason. We all sit here and talk about market structure for a reason. As an example, as a public exchange, and as a displayed market, when you talk about fair access and you talk about our dissemination of data, our responsibility to the marketplace is to ensure that we continue to provide new programs to incentivize liquidity.[19] The liquidity is not just with the high-frequency traders, or HFTs. It's on the retail side. it's on the buy-side. It's created an ecosystem for people to trade, and that's the responsibility of the exchange or any type of liquidity source.

HARTS: I'd agree with that. The competition between exchanges has done amazing things for liquidity and transparency throughout the national market system. As for the question about market makers being there with the continuous, two-sided quote, it's something we think about a lot. The point we always come back to when we're thinking about this is that you have to ask yourself: Compared to what? For example, when we talk about high-frequency traders providing markets today, are they willing to stand in front of an oncoming freight train? Probably not. But compared with the days of 20 or 25 years ago on the floor of the New York Stock Exchange, neither were those NYSE specialists willing to stand in front of an oncoming freight train. There is this popular myth or longing for a time when someone was going to stand there and just buy no matter how fast the market was selling off, no matter how fast it was dropping. It never happened folks; it wasn't there.

Once again, I don't think things are that much different today. If you expect someone to stand there and provide liquidity in rapidly changing markets that are moving against them, you better have really big incentives for them to stand there and do it because otherwise, there is no reason for them to be there.

MAHONEY: I agree 100 percent, having traded through the 1987 crash. But the one thing that the New York did, and only the New York did, was single stock

[19] Reg NMS (Regulation National Market System) was adopted by the Securities and Exchange Commission in 2005 and introduced 2 years later to further advance the ideals of a national market system. The regulation includes the order protection, or trade-through rule; access rule (fair access) to market data including quotations; rules on sub-penny trading and on market data.

dislocation, making it halt the market.[20] But now you felt better about that, right? A lot of it was an emotional reaction. It wasn't just as if I knew what was happening. It stopped the dissemination of information; you would be able to build the book again, and it was a little slow. There was definitely a perception that the outcome was fair or better. I'm not sure if that was necessarily the case if you measured it objectively. But for sure, what the traditional New York specialists did very well was to take the three standard deviation single stock event and do something.

In the big events, say like in 1987, there was nobody who could do anything about that.[21] We were almost at war with Iran. Like everybody forgets, there were rockets being fired in the Gulf. I mean this was a problem. And so the market had run up dramatically, but nobody stopped that.

HARTS: But when we talk about the role of specialists…

MAHONEY: I'm not romanticizing them, trust me.

HARTS: You're talking about this sense of well, they would walk a stock down, and so it would slowly go down, and they had to commit capital at certain price points. And you're right, it made people feel better. There was no dropping off a cliff Flash Crash kind of phenomena.

MAHONEY: We've all tried to do it, but nobody has been able to do it successfully, and it is this: How do we recreate an event where we can somehow force rational behavior into a marketplace that's irrational? The specialists in former times just said, "I have no idea what's going on. I have full authority here. We're not trading, and everybody just stopped." And so they were able to stop those outlier events from occurring. In the end, I'm not sure if the price they restarted trading at was a better outcome than the continuous market walking a stock down. But, for sure, they did force some sort of rational behavior to occur. Look, we all try to do it. Limit up, limit down is an example of that.[22] I mean, we are constantly trying to recreate that. I wouldn't say that was the only good mechanism, or that it was the best mechanism, compared to having a human trading participant in these market situations.

There is this guy, a friend of mine who's in his eighties. I know him from the floor days. The question he always asks me is, Who stops the market when something bad happens? He was a New York Stock Exchange guy, and he would say, "In the old days I knew what to do. We had rules and regulations, but in a fragmented market, there is nobody in command." I don't think most of the time people care, but

---

[20] For more on trading halts in the US markets, see backgrounder on Securities and Exchange Commission: https://www.sec.gov/fast-answers/answerstradinghalthtm.html

See Has Wall Street Employed Enough Tech to Protect Against Another Black Monday? Circuit breakers and tech can safeguard against market meltdowns, but cannot completely prevent market crashes. The Street examines the technology of the era and the technology of today as part of its Black Monday special report. Chris Nolter. *The Street.com* https://www.thestreet.com/story/14345945/1/rebooting-wall-street-technology-after-black-monday.html

[21] See footnote 10. Black Monday.

[22] NASDAQ Frequently Asked Questions: https://www.nasdaqtrader.com/content/MarketRegulation/LULD_FAQ.pdf

in those outlier events, how do we solve them? That's a big mystery in market structure, although not a topic for this panel. But that is still the last piece we need to figure out.

HARTS: People would say that investors are served well with markets that can reflect prices and that they are better off the more efficient and the faster markets are at doing this. I am not sure that you can really make the point that there should be one person in charge of stopping everything.

MAHONEY: It didn't work on August 24th, 2015, when we had big price swings, so we cannot be complacent.

WAELBROECK: Just to clarify, there's actually slightly different processes. If you look at 1929, and 1987, the microstructure of those events is actually very distinct from the 1962 Flash Crash and the May, 2010 Flash Crash.[23] There are different types of physical processes involved.[24] What happened in 1987 and 1929 are more tied to actual macroeconomic or global events. Alternatively, you can have events driven by just fundamental feedback mechanisms in the economic system. We are always at risk of them. But they are not entirely the same or as endogenous as a Flash Crash phenomenon that it is completely driven by the dynamics of algorithms, reacting to other algorithms, or traders reacting to other traders.

MAHONEY: But some of the '87 crash certainly was connected to portfolio insurance, without a doubt. I mean, futures were 5 years old at that point, and none of us knew what was going on.[25]

The selling of futures versus, you're laughing, but I think it was, right? Besides with your Quotron, you were running like 10 minutes late, so who knew what was going on?[26]

WEBER: We're all in agreement that there's been a transformation and lots of improvements because of technology. But it seems like there is still a perception gap out there. If that perception gap drives politicians and regulators, have we really told the full story of market technology correctly? Are we able to let the politicians and the regulators understand that we have gained a lot of advantage from the way we trade today? But then as you were pointing out, Tim, there's nobody there now to say you're accountable for what happened at, say, 9:47 in the morning or 2:37 in the afternoon? How do we improve that perception, and get the story of technology out there better?

WAELBROECK: I'm not going to speak for politicians. But to the extent that the market has been in the critical state, and will always be in the critical state, you

[23] Stock Market Crash of 1929. History Channel. Updated April 6, 2020. https://www.history.com/topics/great-depression/1929-stock-market-crash

[24] Back to the Future: Lessons From the Forgotten 'Flash Crash' of 1962. Jason Zweig. *Wall Street Journal*. May 29, 2010. https://www.wsj.com/articles/SB10001424052748703957604575272791511469272

[25] S&P 500 futures were launched in 1982.

[26] Quotron was the name of the Los Angeles-based company that in 1960 became the first financial data technology provider to send stock market quotes to an electronic screen rather than to a printed ticker tape.

could almost make the argument that it's not all that relevant. There are arguments that features of Reg NMS, enabling ISOs, or Intermarket Sweep Orders, have worsened the situation with microfractures in the market.[27] I think those are viable arguments, and there are no doubt opportunities for regulators to screw things up. But at the end of the day, the markets will organize in a critical state. We will have mini crashes. And the natural stabilizer role is to be played by those in the market community, such as hedge funds with longer-term holdings or other institutional investors who are in the business of trying to identify fair price.

By the way, shortly after say around 2010, we wrote a requirements document titled *The May 6th Requirements* that is still pertinent and maintained.[28] It describes a collection of features that allowed algorithms executing buy orders to take opportunities presented by microfractures automatically in the markets, essentially buying faster when the price has been driven down by one of these events. This kind of algorithmic execution feature is a natural stabilizer for the market. Once techniques like this become more widely adopted, they will reduce the frequency and severity of microfractures by allowing scheduled orders to provide liquidity when it is in high demand. To the extent that practices like this do become more widespread, you'll find that the institutional liquidity fulfills its role as a natural shock absorber and provider of price stability. This is, in fact, when the structure of an event indicates, it is a dislocation and not an information-driven event.[29]

MAHONEY: There is this enormous perception about technology. We've become dependent on technology, and we love it when it works. But when it doesn't work, we immediately become miserable and blame the technology like, "Oh, you know, there's so much on my smartphone when it doesn't work. What am I going to do now?"

We're so dependent on technology in every aspect of our lives today that we've become highly critical of any technology failures. But as somebody who runs a technology company, I'll tell you nothing's perfect. You're going to have breaks here and there, and it's a matter of how quickly you recover and how you minimize the fractures.

We all have to get comfortable with the fact that there will be certain aspects of technology you can't control. It's a matter of can you stop it from occurring again. Can we prevent another May 6th, 2010, Flash Crash event? Well, we did. Can we prevent another August 24th, 2015, event? I'll leave that to others to consider. In any event, we've done a better job at avoiding the next crash, but I'm still not sure.

---

[27] An Intermarket Sweep Order is an order that sweeps across the marketplace, picking up as many shares as possible at the best prices available using an algorithm. It's a sort of digital exception to the "order protection rule" that says orders have to be filled at the lowest possible price.

[28] Referring to the Flash Crash of May 6, 2010. It lasted about 36 minutes, erasing 998.5 points, or about 9% in the Dow Jones Industrial Average, and then quickly recouping the losses as the various indexes rapidly rebounded in this high-speed, electronic trading phenomena. At the time, it was a record one-day point decline on an intraday basis in the history of Dow Jones Industrial Average.

[29] "Natural shock absorber" here refers to being able to absorb the shock of a sharp trading imbalance.

Again, we'll find something else wrong in our market structure that we have to continually fix. I think we're at the same place in our marketplace as the entire world is with technology. It works great, and then we have to keep evolving it. And you only evolve it after something goes wrong.

HARTS: The point I would make here is that the regulation has evolved as a response to the technology, not the other way around. You know, we had ECNs like Instinet, although we didn't call them that back then until the regulators came out and said, "Oh, that's an ECN."[30]

The regulators have done a great job, at least on the equity side, in keeping up with changes in technology. But in general, markets function better when people are free to innovate and to create new systems and new technology for trading. The longer we go down that road, the better off we're going to be.

CHRISTIAN: I agree. From the Street's perspective, and the way we're perceived, availability in the markets is key? Any major event that happens in our markets will be on the front pages of *The Wall Street Journal* and *USA Today*. The perception out there is that we all need to be monitoring and to be aware of technology.

We're now a fragmented market, and competition from fragmentation has allowed for all these various pools of liquidity and multiple exchanges. We have the example of how the NYSE was out of the market for almost 4 hours.[31] That was a kind of event for the broader market space where participants in response went, wow, there are still other markets out there as well, so the market is still working, right?

Technology and regulation allowed that fragmentation to grow. Because stocks continue to trade on other markets, markets continue to work. It is important that we continue to understand that we need to be available for trading. To be available for liquidity. We must take that responsibility seriously. That perception is important.

WEBER: Questions from the audience?

ATTENDEE [Baruch College student]: There seems to be a deep umbilical link between liquidity provision and market structure. We've had Reg NMS and fragmented markets leading to the rise of high-frequency trading. Before that, we had monopolistic markets, dominated by NYSE and NASDAQ, leading ultimately to fragmentation. Do you think the current market structure is ideal? And, say 5 years from now, what big changes do you anticipate in the market structure? Or will there be no changes at all, because the way we are going is just great?

HARTS: There is always room for improvement.

MAHONEY: Former SEC Commissioner Dan Gallagher has always said it best. It's the holistic review. I guess as a practitioner, you always worry about when you make little changes here and there. There are some fundamentals to consider, like

---

[30] Instinet. https://www.instinet.com/

[31] Trading resumes on NYSE after nearly 4-hour outage. Patrick Gillespie, Matt Egan and Heather Long. CNNMoneyInvest. July 8, 2015
https://money.cnn.com/2015/07/08/investing/nyse-suspends-trading/

BATS and BIDS are just fundamentally different but we're regulated differently.[32] And we're similar enough that the way we're regulated probably doesn't make a ton of sense. And so, yes, you can alter ATS rules, and you can close the gap a little bit. But every time Bryan has a good idea, does he have to put it out for public comment? That made sense when it was a monopoly. I don't know if it makes sense now. There's some fundamental change, such as amending parts of the Exchange Act of 1934. That does make sense.

HARTS: But we shouldn't rely on the regulators to legislate market structure. We, as an industry, should be creating the market structure, working with them to make sure it's properly regulated.

MAHONEY: There are certain things we can't change though, like the role of the SRO, the Self-Regulatory Organization. It doesn't make sense to change some fundamental stuff. And some of that is at the Congressional level. In this regard, a holistic review would highlight and point out a bunch of market structure issues and get us to a potentially more interesting spot, because it's hard to have a twenty-first-century market structure where we're holding on to vestiges of the Maloney Act.[33] I am not suggesting that a review is an easy path. It's over 70 years old.

Larry Tabb [TABB Group]: In the last 18 months, the big topic for liquidity has been about speed bumps. Have they been successful or not? What are your thoughts on the speed bumps?[34] Are they better for markets, or are they making things more problematic?

CHRISTIAN: Bill Harts is excited on that one. [Laughter]

HARTS: In case anyone didn't hear, we opposed speed bumps that are designed as an integral part of a market's structure. The reason is simple. We think they have a detrimental effect on the ability to provide liquidity. That's because if a market maker isn't sure of what the right price is amongst all different exchanges, then he or she will have trouble pricing the securities. As it was noted earlier, you have to know what the right price is at any given time, and speed bumps seem to throw a wrench into that. They throw a speed bump into that!

The fact that other markets are now coming out with their own versions of speed bumps—and we've heard talk that there may be even more coming—at the end of

---

[32] BATS is an ATS; BIDS is an ATS.

[33] Maloney Act. The US legislation passed in 1938 that allowed self-regulatory organizations to assist the SEC in some financial regulation. That is, the Maloney Act encouraged what was essentially a public-private partnership between the federal government and the financial industry. Source: freedictionary.com

The NASD was founded in 1939, under provisions of the 1938 Maloney Act amendments to the Securities Exchange Act of 1934. It was also the leading founder of the NASDAQ stock market, which was established in 1971. Investopedia.

https://securitiesce.com/definitions/5834-maloney-act-of-1938/

[34] Exchange Speed Bumps: An Indirect Way to Reduce Buy-Side Trading Costs. Traders Magazine Online News, August 20, 2019. Jeff Bacidore

http://www.tradersmagazine.com/news/ecns_and_exchanges/exchange-speed-bumps-an-indirect-way-to-reduce-buy-side-trading-costs-119893-1.html

the day, we think that will only serve to further complicate the markets. It makes it more difficult to provide liquidity.[35]

MAHONEY: I'd rather end up with the Dave Weisberger idea which is having Securities Information Processors, or SIPs, in each data center.[36] The idea being that speed bumps are a way to solve the SIP versus the direct fee problem. I would rather solve it fundamentally.

There are fundamental things we will have to do to address some of these issues. By not addressing those issues, we add to complexity. If ultimately the speed bump is the way to take away those advantages, how about we just solve it in a more fundamental way, which is the Dave Weisberger SIP idea that is in front of Congress today.

WAELBROECK: In terms of market structure, whatever you throw in, the market participants will find a way to work with it and get the market back to its usual critical state of very thin liquidity. There is another question that concerns me a little bit more. In this very complex market structure that we have today, do we have fair access? Do institutional clients have effective access to the some 135 or so order types now in the US stock market? Or is access effectively restricted to those high-frequency players or high-volume players that have special pipes to the marketplace? There is a fundamental inequity in terms of market access that the regulators could usefully address. Aside from that, we'll figure it out.

MAHONEY: By the way, this all goes back to what we've been talking about—complexity. If an exchange could discriminate between clients and offer alternative access arrangements, there might be a different way to do this. But the fact that we force fair access in a way, has created this complexity that you can't even understand? So it's part of the rule set.[37] If we came up with a better rule set, we might be better off.

WEBER: Bob and Larry, we've got the topic for next year: Speed Bumps, Complexity, and Access to the Markets! [Laughter] I'm going to propose not a speed bump, but a road block, now that we are at the end of our time. Please join me in thanking the panelists for sharing their insights with us. Thank you.

---

[35] More Exchanges Add "Speed Bumps," Defying High-Frequency Traders. Alexander Osipovich. *Wall Street Journal*. July 29, 2019.

[36] Dave (David) Weisberger of HIS-Markit was at this same 2016 Baruch conference, on the panel, What Can Be Done to Drive Mid and Small-Cap Liquidity?

At the time of writing, the Securities and Exchange Commission had formally introduced rule making on geographically diverse SIPS. See p.253 of this SEC rule of 2020. "C. Competing Consolidators." https://www.sec.gov/rules/final/2020/34-90610.pdf

[37] This "fair access" Mahoney is referring to goes back to the Securities Exchange Act of 1934. Unlike a broker, an exchange may not discriminate between members of the exchange. This means an exchange must offer all services to all members with the same fee structure. Brokers who run ATSs, on the other hand, may charge different customers different prices, or even decide not to do business with a given customer at all.

Chapter 3
Liquidity: A Fluid Concept from a European View

Robert A. Schwartz and Rainer Riess

I was invited here today to present my views on the topic of liquidity from a European perspective. My first reaction was undeniably blunt: That's a difficult topic!

Nevertheless, I will begin by briefly talking about liquidity as a concept. By the same token, I am also aiming to present the European perspective. Taking some European time travel, let's call it, from the late '80s through today, I will be noting the changes along the way because of regulation and technology, the implications of that for liquidity, and the impact on our industry. Also, I want to talk about one thing that is a little bit like the elephant in the room when it comes to the future of liquidity—and in my view that is Brexit.[1] At the end, I want to share my overall thoughts and the potential implications at stake.

I'll start with a picture as shown in Exhibit 3.1 that I took 10 days ago in Cuba of the Bolsa de la Habana, once one of the largest stock exchanges in Latin America. Exhibit 3.1 is a picture of no liquidity since 1959![2] The interesting part of that picture is probably not the closed doors of the exchange, because there has been no trading in Havana since the revolution. That, of course, is a societal choice. What do you want to have for a market economy? What are the boundaries around it and so on? All of you are quite aware of that.

[1] Brexit was the departure of the United Kingdom from the European Union at the end of January 31, 2020, with the important arrangements governing that exit taking effect January 1, 2021.

[2] Will stock investors ever profit from a more open Cuba? May 1 2015. Leslie Kramer.*CNBC.com*. https://www.cnbc.com/2015/05/01/investors-ever-profit-from-a-more-open-cuba.html

R. A. Schwartz (✉)
Zicklin School of Business, Baruch College - CUNY, New York, NY, USA
e-mail: robert.schwartz@baruch.cuny.edu

R. Riess
Director General, Federation of European Securities Exchanges (FESE), Brussels, Belgium

R. A. Schwartz et al. (eds.), *Liquidity*, Zicklin School of Business Financial Markets Series, https://doi.org/10.1007/978-3-031-36914-8_3

The very interesting point about that picture is up above the door, on the window, in the middle to be exact. And that's this white sign with a blue anchor on it, which stands for a *casa particular*, a Spanish word which means in English a private hotel or rooms to let. In any event, a market economy is actually finally starting again at the exchange in Havana. I thought that was an interesting development.

For me, the concept of liquidity over the last 30 years has been mysterious because it's really something that is not there when you need it. It tends to be there in over supply when it's not so necessary. So the job of exchanges is how to maintain fair and orderly, and liquid markets.

I will start with another visualization, this time coming from Brussels. The FESE, the Federation of European Securities Exchanges, is domiciled in Brussels.[3] Someone talked about wine and liquidity here today! Well, the Belgians love their beer so when they think about liquidity, our thoughts turn to beer!

What's the concept in terms of liquidity? Clearly, it's the degree to which an asset or security can be quickly bought or sold in a market without affecting the asset's price. You want to have substantial size and a low cost. According to Hasbrouck and Schwartz, it's measured according to four dimensions: market breadth, market depth, immediacy in execution, and market resiliency.[4] And one measure that exchanges in particular very often look at is market impact. That is to say, exchanges really look at what happens when a buyer or seller comes in, and how much the price would move through that investor's order coming in, whether upward or downward. And that is obviously what exchanges try to manage through their work.

Liquidity is the key thing for exchanges. It is the most important decision-making criteria for investors considering whether to buy or sell a security. And it's a central quality characteristic of whether a market is functioning well or not.

At the core, you could say that liquid capital markets are essential for the efficiency of capital allocation. In modern economies, it leads to low costs of capital for the issuer, so there is really price discovery at work. At the heart of it, price discovery is not working in Cuba, a situation which is also a cost factor for Cuba. That is something to remember. Whatever we do, this price discovery process, keeping it active, is probably the biggest asset we, as marketplaces, can provide to the society at large. It increases the overall welfare of society.

On a micro level, this same price discovery dynamic probably enables access to a large number of trading interests and ensures that investors can carry out their transactions at any time. I would dub that idea as resilience. Resilience is how that

---

[3] The Federation of European Securities Exchanges (FESE) https://fese.eu/about-fese/

[4] Liquidity and execution costs in equity markets. Joel Hasbrouck and Robert A. Schwartz. *The Journal of Portfolio Management.* Spring 1988, 14 (3) 10–16; DOI: https://doi.org/10.3905/jpm.1988.409160

https://jpm.pm-research.com/content/14/3/10

liquidity is available at all times and how stable it is. That is extremely important for exchanges to look at and for exchanges to manage.

How do exchanges do it? Starting in the Middle Ages, the story of exchanges is pretty much the same for them all. People gathered to consolidate and concentrate liquidity in one place. For example, in 1585, the Frankfurt Stock Exchange was founded; in 1792, the Buttonwood Tree Agreement, the founding agreement for the New York Stock Exchange, was signed. It always was pretty much the same everywhere, having traders come together to make sure that everybody transacts in the same trading system. Whether that's under a tree or whether that's on an electronic trading venue that has spread over competing markets doesn't really matter; you have to meet and concentrate liquidity. This is why exchanges always try to facilitate the search for liquidity, by concentrating order flow in a single place.

In this regard, a so-called concentration rule arose at the New York Stock Exchange and similar rules emerged in most European countries. Call markets were quite prevalent back in the day. Then, with the advent of technology, a continuous trading environment started to evolve in our markets. We already heard quite a lot about that today at this conference. Exchanges are always faced with a question of how to manage liquidity, how to look for size and depth, and how to manage implicit and explicit transaction costs.[5] Exchanges can do that by various means.

Then there is the role of market makers in the trading systems. That's always about what parameters you set such as tick sizes, and the transaction fees in an exchange is charging. We heard today about access provision, speed bumps, and the like.

Going back again in history, I remember working in 1987 on the floor of the Frankfurt exchange when the crash known as Black Monday happened.[6] We were actually printing the buy and sell orders on pink and white slips at the time. When the crash happened, all of a sudden, the baskets weren't big enough to carry all the orders to the specialists. That's when a revolution was needed, and that's when the advent of electronic trading really began in Europe.

[5] Transaction Costs and What They Mean. State Street Global Advisors. https://www.ssga.com/dc/2017/dc-guide-to-transaction-costs.pdf

[6] "The first contemporary global financial crisis unfolded in the autumn of 1987 on a day known infamously as 'Black Monday.' A chain reaction of market distress sent global stock exchanges plummeting in a matter of hours. In the United States, the Dow Jones Industrial Average (DJIA) dropped 22.6 percent in a single trading session, a loss that remains the largest one-day stock market decline in history. At the time, it also marked the sharpest market downturn in the United States since the Great Depression." Source: Stock Market Crash of 1987. Federal Reserve History. Donald Bernhardt and Marshall Eckblad, Federal Reserve Bank of Chicago. https://www.federalreservehistory.org/essays/stock_market_crash_of_1987

In the late '80s we heard the Big Bang in London, and then it happened here in the United States.[7] Computerization began to take off, and trading anonymously also had a huge impact.[8]

In Europe, the biggest change factor likely wasn't MiFID, or a lot of other things, such as the Big Bang.[9] In my opinion, as shown in Exhibit 3.2 entitled "Regulatory change in Europe," it was the Investment Services Directive, or ISD, in Europe in the 1990s that started the regulatory change in Europe.[10] What did that actually change? The United States had a capital market since the Industrial Revolution, and it was one capital market. So since the 1870s, 1880s, New York was the financial center of the United States. There were of course other regional stock exchanges in the United States. But the United States was one single capital market.

In Europe, up until the late 1980s, we had domestic markets. It was very expensive and difficult to trade in other geographies. To go from London to Frankfurt, from Frankfurt to Paris, was costly and it was difficult. Because of that, trading between the countries was not very large. So definitely, the ISD changed that by allowing what was called remote membership. That meant a London-based trader could become a member of the derivatives markets, or of another trading system, say on the Frankfurt Stock Exchange. A German trader could become a member of the Paris Exchange.

That was complemented a little bit by a regulation that came later, in 2007, the Market and Financial Instruments Directive, MiFID, which I previously referred to. As also shown in Exhibit 3.2, MiFID brought about in Europe the kind of changes

[7] "The Big Bang refers to the day the stock market was deregulated in London, England. The event, in which the London Stock Exchange (LSE) became a private limited company, took place on October 27, 1986. It revitalized the LSE, allowing external corporations to enter its member firms, and an automated price quotation was established.

"Before the Big Bang, the LSE was trailing the other major exchanges in the world. At the time, the New York Stock Exchange (NYSE) was the biggest market worldwide, determined by the turnover rate. London was only able to turn over 1/13 of the volume transacted by the NYSE. The electronic trading system helped improve London's turnover rate because orders were now accepted by telephone and computer."

Source: Investopedia.

https://www.theguardian.com/business/2006/oct/06/usnews.internationalnews

[8] "Anonymous trading occurs when high profile investors execute trades that are visible in an order book but do not reveal their identity. Many stock exchanges, such as the London Stock Exchange, Toronto Stock Exchange, New York Stock Exchange, and NASDAQ, as well as dark pools offer anonymous trading. While most traders choose to trade non-anonymously, there are many reasons that larger traders prefer to keep their participation in a market a secret." Source: Investopedia

[9] Markets in Financial Instruments Directive I, or MiFID I, introduced in October 2010, was followed by the second MiFID proposals, or MiFID II, in September 2012, aiming for the reform and harmonization of European area markets. MiFID II shifts the European regulatory regime from a principles-based to a more US-style, rules-based regulatory model.

[10] THE EUROPEAN UNION'S INVESTMENT SERVICES DIRECTIVE. MANNING GILBERT WARREN III.* Penn Law. Legal Scholarship Repository. Summer 1995. https://scholarship.law.upenn.edu/cgi/viewcontent.cgi?article=1509&context=jil

you also have in the United States, competition between trading venues.[11] With MiFID, the goal was full transparency of what is traded in the European markets. That goal has been partly achieved in Europe.

On the last panel, we heard about the idea of algo trading and HFT boosting liquidity. As shown in Exhibit 3.3, a Bundesbank study of Eurex data for the DAX and bond future trading in 2014 basically concludes that active HFT participants during times of high volatility, as well as when volatility is expected—say when news events you know will happen on a certain day—are really improving price determination.

They are very useful agents in the market in short-term intervals. The same was evident for the non-news events. So if liquidity spiked or if a news event happens that was not announced previously, they would be increasing, significantly, short-term volatility.

On the other hand, passive HFT participants have been found to be often absent in volatile phases and to reduce their liquidity provided. In summary, this same industry examination said active and passive HFT participants overall increased the risk of episodes of short-term excessive volatility, which can lead to market imbalances, and potentially could add to a flash crash scenario.

I would say overall in Europe we've not seen any flash crashes directly. We've not seen major market events like how they played out in the United States. Overall, my assessment is that HFT and algorithmic trading in Europe has significantly helped to increase liquidity; it has significantly helped to lower bid-ask spread and to act as a bridge between fragmented markets.

We don't have Reg NMS in Europe, so there is no European wide best price rule, as each order book really competes in price determination with other order books.[12] You couldn't bridge that fragmentation if algorithmic trading and HFTs were not performing their role in this outcome.

---

[11] Markets in Financial Instruments Directive I, or MiFID I, introduced in October 2010, was followed by the second MiFID proposals, or MiFID II, in September 2012, aiming for the reform and harmonization of European area markets. MiFID II shifts the European regulatory regime from a principles-based to a more US-style, rules-based regulatory model.

[12] Reg NMS vs. MiFID. Regulation National Market System (Reg NMS) and the Markets in Financial Instruments Directive (MiFID) represent major changes in the structure of the markets for equities trading in the United States and European Union (EU), respectively.

https://www.wallstreetandtech.com/trading-technology/reg-nms-vs-mifid/d/d-id/1257816.html#:~:text=Regulation%20National%20Market%20System%20(Reg,European%20Union%20(EU)%20respectively.&text=But%20Reg%20NMS%20is%20more,a%20broader%20range%20of%20issues

European Best Bid and Offer (EBBO) is a regulatory mandate that brokers provide current best prices available for buying or selling financial instruments. EBBO is the European equivalent of the National Best Bid and Offer (NBBO) in the United States. On any exchange, a series of price levels appear for both the buy- and sell-side market. The EBBO represents the best price that is available—the lowest price for a buy or the highest price for a sell. The EBBO continually updates the prices so the market participants have fair access to the best prices to transact trades. European Best Bid and Offer (EBBO). Source: Will Kenton. *Investopedia.* April 4, 2019.

That same system seems to be working very well up to now in increasing liquidity overall. But, of course, there is a little bit of unease. There are investors who simply think, in the wake of the financial crisis and the US Flash Crash, that there's less liquidity out there. The feeling is of less breadth and depth of markets than in the past.

And the claims of unfair markets—we heard the discussion of speed bumps—is very much something resonating in Europe, as well. In Europe, the current debate also goes like this: Do we need a revision of market structure? How can we find a compromise to get a more liquid market again for investors?

But let's look a little bit at what really has happened. I just thought it would be instructive to look at a very, very long timescale. ISD, in the early '90s, really changed something.[13] If you look at Exhibit 3.4, the graph here from Euronext for the top 40 French stocks from 1990 to 2015, something really interesting happens between 1990 and 2000. In these 10 years, you had the advent of electronic trading and ISD. Investors could actually have a pan-European market; they could become active because of these changes. And you see that liquidity in that timeframe somewhere rose between 30 and 50 times. This was unlocking Europe as a capital market for the first time, something that occurred in the United States much earlier, but which really happened in Europe only in the 1990s, up until the year 2000.

The interesting part to the right side of Exhibit 3.4 is that in the graph, even during the financial crisis, you saw liquidity spike. And afterward, the overall liquidity seems to be pretty flat between 2000, 2001, and today.

That is also something that we find in other markets. Here are the results in Exhibit 3.5 from Deutsche Boerse, Bolsa de Madrid, and Euronext, from 2000 through 2014. You see a spike in liquidity in 2006 and 2008. But afterward, liquidity, or overall turnover, seems to go back to a precrisis level.

Here's the other thing and the reason my conclusion is about market quality. Look at the so-called XLM, or Extra Liquidity Measure, as shown in Exhibit 3.6.[14] That's a measure that Deutsche Boerse is using to measure market impact in the stocks. What you do is shoot hypothetical orders of a certain magnitude in the order book. You basically measure the market impact that the order would have cost. And this is for the DAX for a 25,000 euro order entering the order book as in Exhibit 3.6. If you look at that again, we've had a lot of progress from the early 2000s where market impact significantly declined. Since then, the innovation in equity markets in Europe has been more limited. If you look at other markets, London, Paris, or wherever, it would be pretty similar. Since then, innovation or liquidity improvement has not been that significant.

The lessons learned from the European markets are summarized in Exhibit 3.7. As I already said, the market structure has worked well. There have been no major market failures in Europe. We can see that, overall, there is high market resiliency

[13] See footnote 10.

[14] Extra Liquidity Measure: (XLM) https://www.xetra.com/xetra-en/trading/market-quality/xlm-xetra-liquidity-measure. Source: Deutsche Boerse.

and immediacy available in the blue chips. But the liquidity spikes we've seen in 2006 and 2008 were not sustainable. The current liquidity levels seem to be stagnant in the current market structure.

There is definitely less market breadth and depth, and a lot of that is attributed to the lack of transparency in Europe. There is a larger share of trading in dark pools, as well as in systemic internalizers.[15] That, of course, is not providing the transparency needed for price formation to occur quite effectively on the lit markets (this is especially of concern in less liquid stocks).[16] I'm curious to hear what the third panel today will discuss around SME liquidity because that's a big concern in Europe.[17]

As I said before, algorithmic trading and HFTs have been positive overall. But, of course, there are new risks that need to be controlled and monitored. Resilience here is the key question to be asked. How can we keep up resilience? And again, what can we do to increase transparency and help price formation? Price formation for me is probably more the concern, even in the less liquid stocks than in the blue chips. In the blue chips, it works well. In the SMEs, we hear a lot of criticism from institutional investors in Europe that price formation is not working anymore, because such a big share of trading is not on lit markets at this point.

In terms of the perception gap, when investors don't really understand algorithmic trading and what this is doing, let me say this. In Europe, the same is happening a little bit even though I would say the regulators, as well as the lawmakers, already have addressed it. In 2012, the European Securities Market Authority (ESMA) published the so-called guidelines on systems and controls in an automated trading environment. MiFID II will put that into European law.[18] As of 2018, a lot of these rules also will be part of European law. And they will require the testing and registration of algorithms, and so on, simply to allow regulators and market participants to make sure that their systems are working properly and that there's no abuse or unfair practices engaged. That's normal protocol with any innovation. That's good. We found a system where I believe innovation can happen, but certainly, supervision can happen as well. I think people can make sure that this is properly done.

MiFID II is coming in 2018 as is shown in Exhibit 3.8. It's really designed to take account of some of the pitfalls I mentioned, the lack of transparency, and it also

---

[15] MiFID II's Trading Hereafter: Systematic Internalizers & Block Venues: https://flextrade.com/mifid-iis-trading-hereafter-systematic-internalizers-block-venues/Source: Flextrade.

[16] A lit market refers to venues that display the various bids and offers in stocks. By contrast, dark markets, or dark pools, do not display prices.

[17] SME stands for small- and medium-sized enterprises.

[18] GUIDELINES-SYSTEMS AND CONTROLS IN AN AUTOMATED TRADING ENVIRONMENT FOR TRADING PLATFORMS, INVESTMENT FIRMS AND COMPETENT AUTHORITIES.

https://www.esma.europa.eu/document/guidelines-systems-and-controls-in-automated-trading-environment-trading-platforms

Source: ESMA.

incorporates some of the lessons of the financial crisis.[19] It is aiming, of course, to make markets more efficient, more resilient, and especially more transparent.

What are the major changes from a liquidity perspective? The major difference we will see is much more stringent transparency requirements. There will be a lot more limitations on dark trading.[20] There will be, again, a trading obligation on lit venues for certain parts of the market. And that's important, to strengthen price discovery in European markets, especially when we're looking at less liquid instruments.

Basically, the fairly successful model on equity markets will be shifted over to derivatives and to other asset classes. In other words, equity, fixed income, commodities, and derivatives will eventually be subject to a fairly similar and common set of rules. Investors expect that for the equity derivatives market. That should, more or less, be positive. There are no major complaints. The industry has lots of concerns in other places. But as regards the trading rules for equity derivatives, investors are generally happy.

The big concern in Europe is what will happen with fixed income? Because aiming to institute equity type models for fixed income will be a revolution. It hasn't been done on a global basis. On the other hand, maybe, bringing light into the darker fixed-income trading can equally reduce trading costs and increase liquidity, as we've seen in equities.

As I promised in the beginning of my session and as shown in Exhibit 3.9, I will give a very brief commentary on Brexit.[21] We are questioned a lot about what will happen because of Brexit. The text laying out Brexit is lengthy but perhaps our host, Robert Schwartz, will publish a book on Brexit, a book to tell us about what's happening after the referendum on June 23, 2016, when Britain voted to leave the European Union. There's this ominous letter that needs to be sent under the so-called Article 50.[22]

What does Article 50 mean? Article 50 is really only the divorce agreement. It's about how the United Kingdom will leave the EU. What happens to the civil servants who are currently working for the EU who have a UK passport? What happens

[19] The well-documented global financial crisis of 2007 and 2008 tied in the United States to subprime mortgage lending. As a reminder, the fall of Lehman Brothers, a global banking behemoth, in September 2008, almost brought the world's financial system to its knees. The worse recession in 80 years followed, but it took massive amounts of fiscal stimulus in the United States to avoid a downward economic spiral, according to financial historians.

[20] See footnote 16.

[21] See Brexit: New era for UK as it completes separation from European Union. *BBC News*. January 01, 2021.

https://www.bbc.com/news/uk-politics-55502781

[22] Article 50 is the only legal mechanism for a member state of the European Union (EU) to leave. A short paragraph in the Lisbon Treaty agreed by all EU member states in 2009, it sets out the steps a country needs to go through to withdraw from its treaty obligations. Source: https://www.instituteforgovernment.org.uk/brexit/brexit-brief-article-50

to UK citizens living in other European countries? What happens to Europeans living in the United Kingdom? What happens to payments to budget? What happens to participation in agencies? The European Banking Authority of the European Union is currently domiciled in London. Where will it move to?

Article 50 and that ominous letter British Prime Minister, Ms. Theresa May, has said she would send out in March, 2017, is all about the divorce agreement.[23] What nobody has talked about yet—and probably the more important thing—is the new trade agreement under Brexit. How are we actually managing the relationship between the United Kingdom and the rest of Europe? And this is the so-called Articles 216 and 217 of the European Treaty.[24] That is probably the one area that will be of most interest to the exchanges. Ms. May has said she is going to send a letter about this to European leaders, even before national elections are held by some members. We're having elections in the Netherlands; we're even having a referendum now in Italy; we're having elections in France in May; we're having elections in Germany in September.

Theresa May has also said that a core objective for the United Kingdom will be to limit immigration from the European Union. There are many Poles, I think about 3 million, living currently in the United Kingdom. And all of that rhetoric—and, of course, that's political positioning, we know that—but all of that rhetoric, nevertheless, makes a possibility of a hard Brexit, a realistic possibility. That is to say, not having absolution by March, 2019, when the 2 years of a transitionary period are over, more likely. And that's the worst outcome. It will definitely make the United Kingdom poorer; it will definitely make the Europeans poorer. It will make the world poorer.

What's the main question at stake for exchanges? It is, How do we maintain the access for investors, issuers, and intermediaries? Today, that is happening through so-called passporting rights, or under MiFID, and the other regulations.[25] Investors from the EU can access the European markets and vice versa. That is, of course, how the integrated market system today works in the Europe Union.

We don't think much today of where a stock is traded. We don't think much about where it is settled; we don't think much about where the issuer comes from,

---

[23] UK Lawmakers Back Theresa May's March 2017 Brexit Schedule Tim Ross and Alex Morales December 7, 2016, 9:51 AM EST https://www.bloomberg.com/news/articles/2016-12-07/u-k-weighs-swiss-norwegian-style-eu-customs-deals-davis-says Prime Minister Theresa May won lawmakers' backing to trigger the start of Britain's exit from the European Union by the end of March next year after promising to give Parliament the chance to scrutinize her plan first.

[24] Consolidated version of the Treaty on European Union https://www.legislation.gov.uk/eut/teu/attachment/43

[25] Source: legislation.gov.uk

Third-country equivalence in EU banking and financial regulation. https://www.europarl.europa.eu/RegData/etudes/IDAN/2018/614495/IPOL_IDA(2018)614495_EN.pdf. Source: European Parliament.

where the investor comes from, or where the broker sits. That potentially could change with Brexit.

What that could mean for liquidity is shown in Exhibit 3.10. If you look at the percentage of trading volume conducted in the United Kingdom, you realize this is a major market disruption that could potentially happen in as soon as a little over 2 years.[26] That will have a lot of influence on liquidity and on how the market structure will work.

As summarized in Exhibit 3.11, the United Kingdom is definitely the main financial center of Europe today, and it's at the heart of the European financial sector. There's a lot of know-how and expertise there. More than three-quarters of all capital markets business on the equity side is conducted out of the United Kingdom. Unpicking that interdependence will be complex. It will be lengthy and costly. Whatever happens, it will increase the cost of liquidity. That, of course, will raise costs for everybody. It will also mean that the EU-27 will need to think about how to structure their capital markets in the future.[27] With the United Kingdom exiting, a European Union project underway, called the Capital Market Union, will be even more important.[28] This will tackle how to integrate further the capital markets of all members' states, how to facilitate easier access, and how to make SME financing easier. It will be even more important because with the United Kingdom cutoff the sources of funding may suffer in some way. You will need to have a new arrangement in this case.

In conclusion, the big question as Europeans is, "How can we best preserve market integrity and liquidity in our markets so that the function that exchanges have to provide—the efficient and effective risk management and price formation for the real economy—is still being properly provided post Brexit." Certainly, it will be a liquidity shock if this doesn't happen in a well-managed fashion. We trust in our smart politicians to hopefully prove me wrong.

Thank you.

Capital Markets Union. European Commission https://ec.europa.eu/info/business-economy-euro/growth-and-investment/capital-markets-union_en
Source: European Commission

[26] Brexit "big bang" to trigger tectonic trading rift in Europe. EURACTIV with Reuters. December 29, 2020. https://www.euractiv.com/section/economy-jobs/news/brexit-big-bang-to-trigger-tectonic-trading-rift-in-europe/

[27] Number of EU member nations with the departure of former member, the UK.

[28] Brexit makes integrating EU capital markets more urgent, Commission says. Dow Jones. *Reuters*. February 20, 2020.

https://www.reuters.com/article/uk-britain-eu-capital-markets/brexit-makes-integrating-eu-capital-markets-more-urgent-commision-says-idUSKBN20E29W

Exhibit 3.1: Liquidity Is Absent, When the Doors Are Closed!

A mysterious concept:
It is there when you don't need it and it tends to be absent when you most need it.
The job of exchanges is to maintain fair, orderly and liquid markets!

Exhibit 3.2: Regulatory change in Europe …

- 1993 **Investment Services Directive (ISD)** allowed for remote electronic access from all over Europe and beyond, resulting in a strong surge of volumes and a rapid shift to electronic trading
  - Liffe versus DTB: Trading of the Bund future rapidly migrated from pit trading at Liffe to the fully electronic DTB (now Eurex).
  - Electronic CLOB with CCPs were introduced at all major European exchanges.
  - Germany was one of the few markets to keep the legacy specialist system until today, still significantly used for trading of illiquid stocks.
- 2007 **Markets in Financial Instruments Directive (MiFID)** entered into force:
  - Europe opted for a competitive system of independent CLOBs and did away with the concentration rules. No NMS, but rather competing price formation centers.
  - The second promise of MiFiD I to bring complete transparency of what is being trade when and where was not fulfilled: part of the market moved away from exchanges to dark pools and systematic internalizers in order to "gain"

an advantage by not being transparent, price formation consequently suffered and liquidity dropped as a result.

Exhibit 3.3: … and Algotrading and HFT – Boosting Liquidity?
Bundesbank Study from October 2016 (based on Eurex data for DAX and Bund future trading 2014)

- Active HFT participants trade more during times of high volatility as well as when volatility is expected (news events), improving price determination in short time intervals as well as increasing significantly short-term volatility.
- Passive HFT participants very often are absent in volatile phases and reduce their liquidity provided.
- In summary, active and passive HFT participants increase the risk of episodes of short-term excessive volatility, which can lead to market imbalances and potentially could aid flash crash situations.

In European markets …

- Algorithmic trading and so called High Frequency Trading (HFT) improved market liquidity by lowering bid-ask spreads and bridging between fragmented markets.
- But the financial crisis, the US flash crashes and the feeling of many investors to have less "liquidity" soon prompted claims of unfair markets.

Exhibit 3.4: Macro View – Turnover CAC 40 from 1990 to 2015

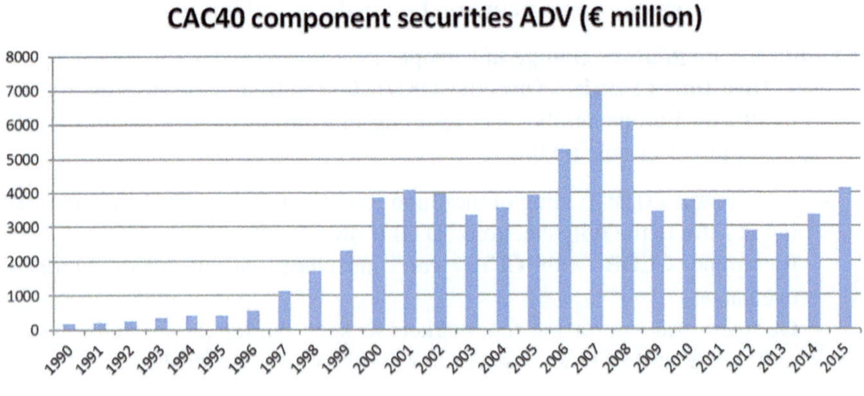

Source: Euronext

Exhibit 3.5: Macro View: European Liquidity 2000 to 2014

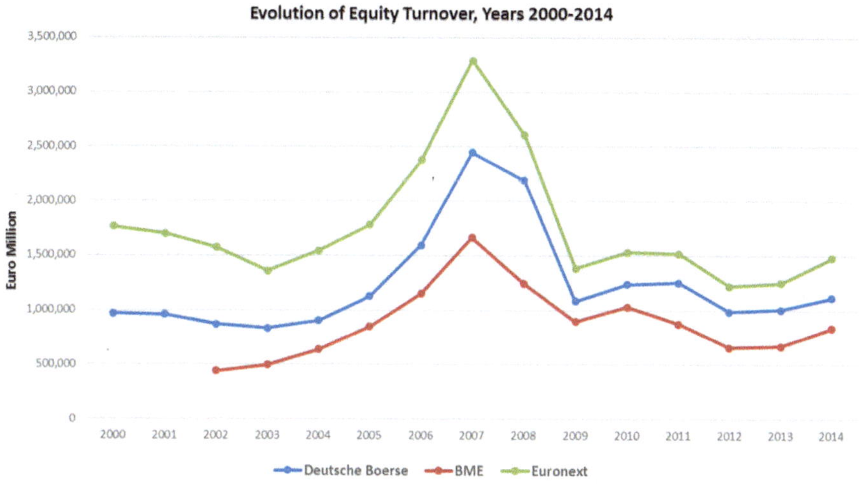

Source: FESE Monthly Statistics

Exhibit 3.6: Micro View: European Liquidity 2000 to 2014

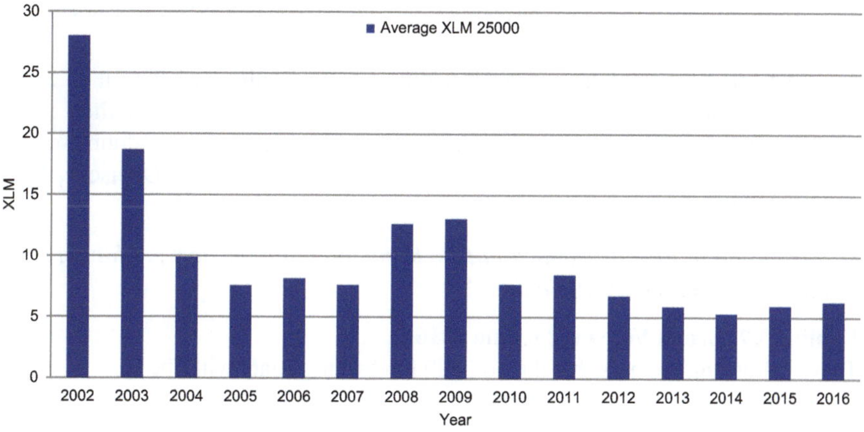

XLM is the Xetra Liquidity Measure. The above graph gives the market impact in bp for the DAX for a hypothetical order of 25000 €.

Source: Deutsche Börse

Exhibit 3.7: Lessons Learned in the European Market

- European equity and derivatives market from 2000 to today worked well, no major market failures like the US flash crashes, and overall high market resiliency and immediacy.

- But liquidity spikes seen in 2006–2008 could not be maintained; current liquidity levels seem stagnant.
- Market breadth and depth have suffered, since dark trading has significantly increased.
- Algorithmic trading and HFT have been overall positive, but create new risk that need to be monitored and controlled.
- All of the above is true for Blue Chips, but less liquid stock have suffered more through in transparency of markets/dark pool trading.

- In 2012 ESMA published guidelines "Systems and Controls in an Automated Trading Environment". MiFiD II will codify these guidelines into European law.
- MiFID II is designed to take into account the lessons learned from MiFID I and the financial crisis, and how to improve the functioning of financial markets making them more efficient, resilient, and transparent.

Exhibit 3.8: Liquidity Reloaded: MiFID II?

- **MiFID II changes:**
  - Stringent transparency requirements and limitations of dark trading. Trading obligation on lit venues.
  - Expanding the successful model in equity markets as well as Exchange-Traded Derivatives to all asset classes (equity, fixed income, commodities, and derivatives).
  - Liquidity for equity and derivatives markets is expected to develop positively.
  - Fear by some that MiFiD II in fixed-income and OTC derivatives may prove detrimental for liquidity. "The liquidity situation is already bad as it is …. we have to leave good investment opportunities on the table because there is not enough liquidity to put the trades on. Transparency can be a double-edged sword" (Juan Landazabal, head of fixed-income trading at Deutsche Asset and Wealth Management).

- ***Revolution in Fixed-income finally to bring light into the dark, reducing trading costs and increasing liquidity?***

Exhibit 3.9: Brexit Vote on 23 June 2016 …

Two separate agreements that the UK will have to negotiate with the EU:

1. Withdrawal Agreement (under Art. 50 TEU)

   - Ending UK contributions to and receipts from the EU budget
   - Catering for the acquired rights of British nationals resident in other EU states, and of EU citizens living in the UK
   - Managing the withdrawal of British civil servants working in the EU institutions
   - Preparing for the exit of British members from the European Parliament, European Court, Committee of the Regions, Economic and Social Committee, etc.
   - Relocating EU agencies out of the UK – notably the hotly sought-after European Banking Authority

- Drawing down UK military involvement from common security and defense policy missions, pulling UK police out of Europol, and ending engagement in Frontex
- Establishing new forms of frontier control, not least at Britain's land borders in Northern Ireland and Gibraltar

2. New Trade Agreement (under Art. 216 and 217 TFEU)

- Current stance of the UK government makes hard Brexit more likely, i.e., a period between the withdrawal and the trade agreement coming into effect, the WTO rules would apply.

- **For exchanges the main questions will be access of investors, issuers, and intermediaries to their services from the UK and into the EU27. Losing passporting rights (with the UK currently accounting for three-quarters of all passporting in the EU) would be a severe disruption to the way markets operate today. And some players like BATS have already announced their plans to consider moving to an EU location.**

Exhibit 3.10: Liquidity After Brexit

UK share of financial markets in the EU

	% share of UK	Date
Hedge fund assets[1]	85	2015
Foreign exchange trading	78	Apr-2013
Interest rate OTC derivatives trading	74	Apr-2013
Marine insurance premiums	65	2014
Fund management	50	2014
Private equity funds raised[1]	49	2014
Equity market capitalisation (LSE)	30	2015
Bank lending	26	2014
Financial services GDP	23	2014
Insurance premiums	22	2014
Banks assets[1]	21	2014
Financial and professional services employment	15	2014

[1] % share of Europe
Source: Various sources; TheCityUK estimates

Exhibit 3.11: Liquidity After Brexit?

- The UK as the main financial center in the European Union today is the center of the continent's financial sector, and we rely on London as a place to do business. London has a huge pool of know-how and expertise when it comes to equity financing.
- More than three-quarters of all capital markets business in the EU27 today is conducted out of the UK. Unpicking this interdependence will be a complex, lengthy, and costly process.
- In any case added complexity will most likely raise costs: banks, venture capitalists, private equity firm, institutional investors, and issuers will face most likely added and new complexities. Bank credit and bond and equity financing on the margin are likely to become more expensive.

- Current efforts in the EU of a Capital Market Union (CMU to encourage the development of deeper and more efficient capital markets and to reduce the dependence of the European economy on bank lending) could be significantly disrupted with big implications for markets participants, investors, issuers, and the economy in the UK and the rest of the EU.
- **The bigger price for all of us: How can we best preserve market integrity and liquidity in our markets in order to ensure the most efficient and effective risk management and price formation in the real economy?**

Chapter 4
What Can Be Done to Drive Mid- and Small-Cap Liquidity?

Robert A. Schwartz, Justin Schack, R. Cromwell Coulson, David Firmin, Jim Ross, and David Weisberger

JUSTIN SCHACK: This panel is titled, "What Can Be Done to Drive Mid- and Small-Cap Liquidity?" To that end, the topic is broken into three sections. First, we ask, Is there a problem right now with small- and mid-cap liquidity? The answer, I suspect, is that we could always use more liquidity. Then, we'll examine some of the reasons why we don't have as much liquidity as we would like. And finally, we'll examine what we can do about that.

I've told the panelists I expect to do as little talking as possible, so they can take and run with our topic. I'll be the liquidity provider of last resort, if you will, and make sure we cover all the ground we're supposed to cover!

Let's start with that first question. Is there enough small- and mid-cap liquidity? Do we have a problem with it?

CROMWELL COULSON: Our market, that is OTC Markets Group, in the off-exchange market, is an interesting place to look at because trading in small companies primarily comprises the activity of individuals, smaller institutions, and family offices.

R. A. Schwartz (✉)
Zicklin School of Business, Baruch College - CUNY, New York, NY, USA
e-mail: robert.schwartz@baruch.cuny.edu

J. Schack
Rosenblatt Securities, New York, NY, USA

R. Cromwell Coulson
OTC Markets Group, Inc., New York, NY, USA

D. Firmin
Instinet Inc., New York, NY, USA

J. Ross
CODA Markets, Glenview, IL, USA

D. Weisberger
IHS-Markit, New York, NY, USA

R. A. Schwartz et al. (eds.), *Liquidity*, Zicklin School of Business Financial Markets Series, https://doi.org/10.1007/978-3-031-36914-8_4

There has been an incredible change in our marketplace in the last 15 years, a change driven by data and technology. The investor experience is vastly improved. Today's E*Trade platform, for example, is better than the professional trader's terminal I had when I came into the industry. Today, the electronic transaction processing power is so much better, and spreads are much tighter.

As I look back at the work we've focused on, it is the online broker and the market maker relationships that we've been helping to facilitate. That focus, in turn, has created a better investor experience for trading these securities.

As for institutions, because we support a range of companies across the liquidity spectrum, it can be a struggle to quickly trade small-cap securities with lower natural trading activity if they don't trade much. In the small-cap market, if you want to quickly exit large-sized positions, you will probably have to take it to a new price to attract a larger group of buyers. In that sense, as you move down the liquidity spectrum, it takes longer to exit a position without a market impact. And that's how securities markets work.

At a high level, I would say that we've created a fantastic investor transactional experience for smaller trades. Market structure is pretty good in terms of small-cap companies. However, if we want to change the overall liquidity dynamic for small-cap companies, we should really talk about how to support stronger retail investor interest—which is the source of greater liquidity—and improve access to capital.

Here's what has happened. We have a regulatory environment that has restricted public companies from efficiently accessing capital. It is easier and more cost-effective to raise capital privately than through public offerings. That is the number one problem because when you raise capital privately, there is limited public transparency, little investor visibility, and no educational marketing. And if you look at exchange-listed small-caps, or at the smaller companies in our space, they're raising capital from shelf offerings, PIPES, or private investments in public equity and discounted private placement shares.

In his recent testimony to the Senate, Steve Lubrello, the SEC Trading and Market Director, noted how for an average $100 million NASDAQ-listed company, 80 percent of the investor base are individuals. Because of current SEC regulations, most individual investors cannot participate in the private market. So we have a gap between the company's seeking capital and their investor base of small individual investors. Since there is no marketing to the natural buyers— that is, to these small individual investors in the secondary market—financing is only available to smaller public companies from PIPES investors and discounted private placement shares.

If we want to focus on how to fix issues of increasing liquidity and creating more public offerings, then we need to modernize regulations for capital raising so that small-cap companies can sell shares directly into the markets. If a company is public, it should not be crimped by regulation to do efficient public offerings.

On the positive side, change is starting to take place because the JOBS Act empowered online securities offerings.[1] However, it is early days and the regulations

[1] Jumpstart Our Business Startups (JOBS) Act https://www.sec.gov/spotlight/jobs-act.shtml

are still too cumbersome. Over the long term, online funding portals will totally transform capital raised in the next 5 years for small companies.

In fact, the benefits of technology will improve access to capital in the same way that Amazon changed how we buy books. Consumers want to shop, so in this regard, investors should be no different than other classes of consumers, when it comes to how an online process is approached for companies selling shares.

Of course, speaking of technology, there are some who say crowd funding is risky. That's similar to what has already been said in the past about E*Trade. These same naysayers make you feel it is much better to have you talk to your broker and pay him $500 at a turn. Yet, if we make it work, crowd funding will totally change secondary markets for smaller companies.

SCHACK: Let's get back to the private versus public debate. I'd also like to hear from the rest of the panel, particularly about the NMS securities world, the small- and mid-cap exchange-listed stocks. Is there a liquidity problem with those names right now?

WEISBERGER: The market structure certainly has pushed us toward and bifurcated the market. There is, in effect, two sets of bifurcations, which I will get into here.[2] Let's look at the individual versus the institutional investor where one bifurcation has occurred. The retail investor is serviced pretty well on the small- and mid-cap companies' side, with a high percentage of retail participation in these securities. The data are extremely conclusive for wholesalers in terms of spreads collapsing and by other measurements. But all of this has bifurcated the market. What you could once do as an institution within your workflow is very, very hard to do today.

Tim was talking about that on the previous panel. In the past, the portfolio manager, the PM, would say, "Okay, I want to buy a sizable position." In a company that's worth, say, $200 million, a sizable position could require four days' worth of trading. And the PMs may have said, "Well, I don't know what this price will be." They have an idea that if they can get it done within a dollar of where it is, the PM would do it, and they may have found out that the bid offer spread on the stock was, say, 10 cents, or 15 cents, something like that. But there's only 100 shares available on the lit markets and yet they need to buy 250,000.[3] So that PM's trader was set up to call a broker, to figure out what he or she could get done in 250,000 shares. Perhaps they'd get started with 100,000. Today, however, they can't do that. And the reason is because when Reg NMS was put in place, there was no block exemption.[4]

[2] Weisberger outlines the market bifurcation as it impacts retail and institutional investors. The other "bifurcation" is, in effect, the transformation that has occurred over time, and as a result of market structure changes, in the trading of small-, mid- and large-cap stocks for institutional investors.

[3] A lit market refers to venues that display the various bids and offers in stocks. By contrast, with dark markets, or Dark Pools, do not display prices.

[4] This refers to how the Reg NMS Order Protection Rule forced orders to be traded at the best possible NBBO price, before getting prices from further down the book.

At the time, it was always amusing. I think I said the same thing at a previous Baruch conference. The idea was, oh, well you could stop people out, meaning that the dealer could turn around and say, "Well, I'll give it to you at this price as a high."[5] But, you know, that was the same thing as giving them the price.

It turns out that dealers who did that went out of business, or at least the people who did it got fired. Because essentially what they were doing was giving pricing that is effectively an option, which is the same as pricing liquidity.[6] Because when you tried to give that price, essentially, sometimes you win, sometimes you lose. And that's okay, the average was to that price. But when you do it as an auction, guess what, sometimes you lose and, well, sometimes you do lose![7] Because the "win" went to the client. And so the price of capital just went way up. And worse, in Reg NMS, there is no ability to delay the print.[8] So not only did you print to the price, you got to see where it would go when it was dealer capital. But the entire world knew the size of your position because they could see the print. They could see what got done, and you could read the tape, as well as every, I hate to call them high-frequency trader. But, let me say, every statistical trader, anyone who has "paid for the tape," can now know exactly what your position is.[9]

---

[5] Put another way, the sell-side broker would set and sell at a "maximum" price in consideration of the block size at stake, trading through the quote—the NBBO—to a specific "stop" limit. That made the broker the counterparty to the trade and it constitutes risk.

See Rule 611, Reg NMS https://www.sec.gov/spotlight/emsac/memo-rule-611-regulation-nms.pdf

See paper Rule 611, Reg NMS. https://www.sec.gov/spotlight/emsac/memo-rule-611-regulation-nms.pdf

Some market analysts have argued that Rule 611 has hurt institutional investors that need to trade in large size, by forcing them to access small-sized quotations, thereby signaling their trading intentions to short-term proprietary traders. Institutional investors typically need to trade in large size. If the market can infer their trading intentions from their trading activities before the full size of their trading interest is executed, the likely result will be an unfavorable price move against the institutional investor, a phenomenon known as "price impact."

To minimize this price impact, institutional investors often seek to execute their orders by splitting them into many, smaller-sized "child" orders that are fed into the market over time.

[6] As referenced previously, the broker taking the other side of a block trade has to, in effect, "set a price limit" to get this block done. That is "market making," in essence, taking on risk as a counterparty. Because before that broker can trade him/herself out of that block position, the price could move against him/her—sometimes significantly—and the broker would take a loss.

[7] Because the trade has to be printed to the tape, that price at that quantity is now public and potentially (and oftentimes) massively impacts the NBBO. "In order to mitigate the risk of losses like this, brokers will then react by make their block 'prices' much more favorable to themselves (unfavorable to the PM/Trader), which makes the block trade more 'expensive' to the buy-side trader/PM and ultimately impacts their performance," according to one market participant.

[8] Reg NMS (Regulation National Market System) was adopted by the Securities and Exchange Commission in 2005 and introduced 2 years later to further advance the ideals of a national market system. The regulation includes the order protection, or trade-through rule; access rule (fair access) to market data including quotations; rules on sub-penny trading and on market data.

[9] The speaker is referring to how market makers and stat arb traders buy "superfast feeds" to the tape so they can watch for price "dislocations" and changes in "fair value," since those "discrepancies" in the spread are how they make money.

Take a poll in a room of traders, buy-side, sell-side, or any side, and ask: "How comfortable are you owning a large chunk of a volume of a stock, or being short that and having every other smart trader know exactly what your position is?" You're not going to get a lot of, "Oh, that's fine, you know." It's not nice and fine like the typical year-round temperatures in San Diego, right? That's a real problem. And that's what Reg NMS did to small and mid-cap liquidity.

On the flip side, if you are incredibly patient, in the aggregate, it looks okay. I know KCG has have published studies saying that it's more or less proportionate throughout the market, that you can get done more or less what you used to be able to get done; you just can't get it done as immediately. And by immediately, that means you used to be able to put risk to the brokers, and the portfolio manager did what he did. It would be necessary to either facilitate that to happen again, that is, put those exemptions back in, go to a more dealer market, or do the Vulcan Mind Meld on every portfolio manager to say you don't need immediacy! Instead, you need to be thinking about the price throughout the day in real time, and re-optimizing your portfolio.[10] In which case you're fine.

SCHACK: That sounds a lot like the way the markets, in general, have changed, forget about just small- and mid-caps. It's sort of like the Flash Boys' problem where, somebody pressing the button expecting to get 500,000 shares done all at once in 2008, or 2009, or 2010.[11] That was kind of a silly thing to try to do.

WEISBERGER: Do you really want me to answer that? Enough people in this room have heard that diatribe. The reality is this: If you smart order route and there's a displayed liquidity, you can get it. But people trying to buy more than the displayed liquidity is something else. A story related to this phenomenon is funny. Someone once asked me what stat ARB was. That someone was Chuck Prince who then was CEO of Citigroup. He asked what stat ARB is the first time I ever met him, since I was running stat ARB at the company. And I looked at him and responded, "Chuck, stat ARB is essentially the art and science of detecting when other people in the market do stupid things to cause mispricing!" We're talking here about stupid

[10] Dealer market in this case refers to a return to a more principle trading-based marketplace where the sell-side is a price-setting counterparty to the buy-side.

In the popular *Star Trek* television series, the Vulcan Mind Meld happened when a Vulcan (like the character Spock) touched another person and pushed his thoughts into their head *(does not apply here but he could also pull the other person's thoughts out!)*. Another similar metaphor from sci-fi films is the *Jedi Mind Trick* from Star Wars. That is where Obi Wan Kenobi convinces the Storm Troopers that "these are not the droids (they) are looking for...."

In summary, Weisberger seems to be saying that the world has changed for the buy-side because it cannot have simple "immediacy" and get bespoke prices anymore. Since the buy-side can't relive this past, it needs to adjust its thinking about the value of blocks. Weisberger's citation of the KCG study was a reference to the fact that performance, by some measures, has actually improved post Reg NMS, because spreads have narrowed. Therefore, even though PMs/traders must spread their executions across lots of small orders, versus one big block, they are arguably getting equal if not better performance.

[11] See Flash Boys: A Wall Street Revolt. Michael Lewis (2015, WW Norton & Company, LLC).

things such as trying to buy 500,000 shares at a split second when there's only 10,000 shares available.

SCHACK: Dave, I'm wondering, is it just a matter of changing your behavior, or are your outcomes worse, even if you do change your behavior, post-NMS? Never mind post-decimalization and the other rules that came before NMS that really changed the old way of providing liquidity. Do we have a bigger problem to try to fix than we might think?

WEISBERGER: I want to tee up Jim Ross for a second. I know what he wants to say. But I'm going to contextualize it.

JIM ROSS: Thank you.

WEISBERGER: It depends on who "they" is. If "they" is the portfolio manager who has handed an order off to a trader, yes. If the "they" is a trader who has been given an instruction from a portfolio manager, they have a very, very, very hard job today, because it doesn't map the previous workflow for someone who wants to commit and trade a large part of it.

Now that said, there are innovations and things designed to do that.

ROSS: My view on the mid- to micro-cap debate is this: I don't think we've ever had a very effective market, especially for the mid- to micro-cap stocks. And this goes back decades. We heard in the past, the previous panels even talked about it, that there's kind of a two-tiered market, if you will. We've certainly done a great job for the large caps. We heard it on the ETFs even, and the top 20 percent of the large-cap stocks trade great. But the other 1880, or whatever the total universe is, are illiquid.

We still must figure out and solve that problem. We've had a bit of a technology tsunami. Alongside regulation, we must find a way to create a market model that works better. Let's try and put the technology applications in there to make this work. We still face the reality that an illiquid doesn't trade well. And it's very hard to put up a block anywhere that may be outside the NBBO.[12]

It's not like in former times, when we had a better opportunity to trade a large block of stock with the dealer and capital commitment, even though that was not always optimal. But it was better than today's markets where that is not an option.

The issue then goes back to the problem. And the problem is our singular reliance on a continuous auction market model, the fact that today we still have pinging, probing, reverse engineering and the issue of market impact.

These [impacts] are decades old, nothing has changed. And now with fragmentation we have probably the bigger issue of delay where there isn't enough liquidity in the market. Put simply, today it takes longer to get your stuff done. And, by the way, you have to show hundred share trades when you are completing a large trade today, and this creates a footprint of your activity for other participants to observe.

[12] National Best Bid and Offer (NBB0). "National best bid and national best offer means, with respect to quotations for an NMS Security, the best bid and best offer for such security that are calculated and disseminated on a current and continuing basis by a plan processor pursuant to an effective national market system plan." Source: Code of Federal Regulations/C.F.R. § 600(b) (42).

We've really made it much more difficult for us to solve the real problem, that is, understanding the actual market model that we rely on. And, because of the diversity of stocks we have, the tick pilot made a mistake because of its one-size-fits-all approach.[13]Every stock has a different dynamic, a different relationship, and each needs to be able to find its own pricing levels and liquidity levels. We don't have a market that allows for that.

Part of this includes not just the market structure but also this relationship between lit markets and dark markets.[14] And we've gotten over the high-frequency trading is bad talk out there, or at least I hope so! But we should and we must also get over this idea that dark is a bad thing for our marketplace. I will argue probably a little bit later that actually a non-displayed market may be a better place for price discovery than a truly completely lit one.

SCHACK: It sounds like there is some consensus that there are improvements that could be made in this area. We talked a little bit about what some of the root causes are. Dave, you brought up NMS and the lack of a block exemption. Jim, you hinted a bit at the idea that trying to set out specific criteria for a large group of stocks is maybe not the best way to go about things.

I want to broaden that idea out a little bit. Are there things that we could or should be doing, that would get around this one-size-fits-all market structure that we have? That is to say, where, for example, hyper-liquid giant capitalization securities trade under the same market structure as small-, mid-, and micro-cap NMS-listed securities? Is that something that we should be attacking? Is that one reason why liquidity is not as good as it should be for the smaller names?

COULSON: Actually, we've had a very matching engine-centric market structure. And that's the great technology available if there are a lot of orders. What's interesting about matching engines is that, in essence, you get what is available on the order books when you submit your trade. Any market maker with an order management system also has an internal matching engine. That infrastructure has emerged through FINRA rules of customer order protection. With order protection, investors are getting that same matching order price priority from broker-dealer order books. But dealers' platforms aren't limited like exchange matching engines. They can create liquidity for orders after they arrive to provide enhanced executions for investors.

As a comparable example, you can look at Tesla, an innovator in the automobile industry, that did away with parking lots filled with unsold cars. That's because Tesla is all about driving orders into their system so that they can create cars in real time. We've been doing that in the securities industry for years; it's called dealer internalization.[15] Here's how that works in practice: A dealer looks at what the

[13] See Investor Alert. Tick Size Pilot Program. What Investors Need to Know. Securities and Exchange Commission. October 03, 2016. https://www.sec.gov/oiea/investor-alerts-bulletins/ia_ticksize.html

[14] See footnote 3.

[15] See Your Broker's Choice. Trade Execution: Jan. 16, 2013 Securities and Exchange Commission. https://www.sec.gov/reportspubs/investor-publications/investorpubstradexechtm.html

market is so that they can provide investors more liquidity and price it more efficiently. If the market price doesn't work for the demand, orders are routed to competing markets until the market gets to a price where buying and selling interests are balanced. The competing dealer model, in a well-regulated market, serves to increase execution quality.

My concern with the tick pilot was this: It became a rule to protect the legacy exchange business model and artificially widen spreads. It did not increase liquidity or improve executions for investors displaying limit orders. Part of the challenge is that exchanges demonize off-exchange trading volume, which makes it hard to discuss how we can help improve the dealer model.[16] With all these online brokers choosing to send their market orders that are seeking liquidity to competing dealers, we should always work to improve dealer liquidity provision and execution.

On the institutional side, I'd flip it. It is "how can institutions help the dealers?" The dealers aren't going to fill large-size trades at prices that market liquidity does not support. How can you participate if you're an institution? Joining dealer liquidity networks is the place where you're going to be able to get more size done.

DAVID FIRMIN: You don't think, though, that you're seeing far less capital commitment in the markets now?[17] I don't like to use the term HFT either, but you're finding some of the faster guys crowding out a lot of that incentive for broker-dealers to actually deal. And they're just ending, up, in effect, merely as brokers.

COULSON: That is all about incentivizing more liquidity provision if you have a trade where you have a customer order, classically called the "tail trade" where a broker-dealer sends the first leg into the market and fills the remainder. That incentivizes temporal liquidity, without the market seeing the full trade. Done by a good trading partner, execution quality is improved, and the post-trade data will expose trading partners to be avoided in the future.

Across equity markets, we have made the execution process faster, and spreads are tighter, so the liquidity that dealers are providing is in smaller amounts. We shouldn't look at them as liquidity providers; they're price setters. Their job is to move the market to the right price where it will trade based on the fundamentals,

[16] Exchanges have long made the case that all volume should migrate to exchange platforms to foster narrower quoted spreads and more liquid markets, according to one market structure analyst.

However, this analyst contended that even with today's debate about price improvement and off-exchange trading, the exchanges "are claiming that actual price improvement provided by off-exchange wholesalers would be reported as much lower if retail volume flowed to exchanges. And if it did, it would tighten spreads, leading to better prices for non-retail participants."

The analyst went on to say that the other side of the argument from dealers like Virtu, Citadel, et al. is that this is just another "self-serving hypothesis by the exchanges, designed to increase their market share."

The analyst added: "No one has proven that more volume on exchanges would be better for the entire market, and it would certainly be worse for retail."

[17] The views and opinions expressed by David Firmin herein are solely his own and do not necessarily reflect the views, opinions, or policies of his employer at the time this recording was made, Instinet, LLC.

meeting the supply and demand and moving prices to the level that balances those forces. That's their job.

The market price setting mechanism needs intermediaries. Dealers are not supposed to go home with inventory. Their job is to get to a price where a maximum of buyers and sellers will trade. They are not long-term position holders. They are price setters and execution providers.

ROSS: I'm sorry. The idea that we have to reimagine a way to offer liquidity incentives for the dealer model so the dealers can make money and provide liquidity is complicated. We have to be careful not to undermine market structure.

COULSON: I don't think we should favor dealers. Agency brokerage is a good deal; we also want proprietary trading, too. And we should be agnostic. We should have auctions and dealer markets. Let's all be open to whatever model attracts customers and not make regulatory choices for investors. Let the market participants choose where they route, and let's provide a level playing field for agency brokers, market makers, alternative trading systems, and exchanges to compete.

ROSS: Right, exactly. But the idea of trying to protect legacy exchange models to force the flow back onto a model that is either market maker or specialist driven is, I think, anathema to the entire institutional kind of direction that we're going. The idea here is that we don't need a dealer any longer to always stand and be there for us. We've got an awful lot of liquidity obviously that's already in the market. What we don't do a very good job of is using market models that help aggregate that liquidity.

We don't need dealers today like we once did historically in the earlier times. That's because there is a lot of flow out there today with billions of shares now trading a day. We can now do a lot of natural matching which occurs in dark pools, and in the market in general. It doesn't have to be the case that the dealer is the first stop for market participants. Naturals, for example, can pair off each other and find each other first. And as I said, my point on the regulatory and the technology front is we have done a great job of putting tape over the holes and the dikes in the continuous market. And we haven't solved the problem that the dike has got cracks in it.

There are inherent weaknesses in the continuous market model, which is to say the bilateral, sequential market that utilizes the quote-driven model to effect liquidity in stocks, small- to mid-cap to large blocks. They do not work well.

It is a fundamental issue about market design. Institutions want to go into the marketplace and meet up with other institutions as best they can naturally. Once they have satisfied that, or want to find more liquidity, they can go to the dealer market. Institutions want to trade with other institutions and have been stymied in an effective way. And we realize that the result is a low hit rate. Therefore, institutions want to find other opportunities in the marketplace. Our market model needs to be adaptive and more forward thinking, rather than going back to an old market maker model.

COULSON: My perspective is that we should all have a level playing field for different business models to compete for trade volumes. When I have visited the Securities and Exchange Commission, I have had staffers ask, "How do we move to an exchange matching engine model?" It has been a consistent point. But I have a different perspective. If you look at it from a regulatory standpoint, competing market makers are messy. Moving trading to fewer centralized matching engines is so much easier to regulate. It is a simple model, with price-time priority, and trading in an orderly and understandable manner.

Has anybody ever seen an item on eBay that you would have liked either to trade at a really cheap price or to sell at a very expensive price? Does that urge make you not want to go there? Or, do you say, "Wow, I missed that opportunity, I should participate more?" It's those kinds of opportunities and situations that we must keep in mind, as our markets move faster, and in which we will have some flash crashes or surges that happen every once in a while. Investors must change their habits and perhaps be more careful in using market orders. But those type of moments are actually opportunities for capital.

I don't think we want to make our markets boring. We should have markets that provide opportunities for everyone to participate on a level playing field. We should let people choose whatever model works, that thrives, and drive the transparency where they can go to get their best execution because not everybody has the same goals on each execution.

SCHACK: Let me see if I can bridge this bid ask spread a little bit here and maybe move the conversation forward on the different ways to provide liquidity. Jim, you talked about institutions, trading with institutions on the one hand, and that is, of course, a very low hit rate. There's a number of platforms that try to do that, and none of them has a particularly large market share. They probably never will the way that our market structure has changed.

On the other side of the coin, we have automated prop shops that are in the business of systematically putting bids and offers into the marketplace, and they are the new generation of a dealer, if you will.

You may disagree on the semantics, whether it's providing liquidity or setting price. I happen to believe that they are committing risk, and that involves providing liquidity, and maybe the buy-side are really the ones who set the price. The fact is most of these firms are trading in very small sizes with very short durations and with some exceptions, concentrating on the higher end of the liquidity spectrum.

Is there a way to get those types of firms more interested in being dealers in those names? I mean, theoretically, the tick pilot is one, and we must talk about the tick pilot even though that's been talked about to death for the last 3 years. But are there other ways besides that?

WEISBERGER: There's a false premise there though, Justin. Here's the funny thing. One of my many jobs over a long career in the industry—and sometimes when I talk to some of the people in this room, it reminds me of just how long that is—was as the architect of the Smith Barney market making system before decimalization was introduced.[18] And this idea, that market makers prior to the order

[18] "A system in which the price of a security is quoted using a decimal format rather than fractions. For example, a decimal trading quote would be $56.25; using fractions, the same quote would appear as $56¼. The US Securities and Exchange Commission (SEC) ordered all stock markets within the US to convert to decimals by April 9, 2001. Prior to 2001, markets in the United States

handling rules and pre-decimalization were incredibly profitable when they interacted with humans looking at their sheets, is a fiction.[19] The fact is if it wasn't for the preopening orders that they had, and their market share, at least in the case of Salomon Smith Barney—because Salomon had Jack Grubman—then it would be another matter.[20] Those guys didn't make money when you took the opening out of the equation. They weren't making money during the rest of the trading day. What were they doing? They were basically making sure their market share was sufficient and big enough so that the investment bankers could convincingly say, "Hey, we want to get any secondary activity. We want to get the IPOs."[21] In that sense, a lot of cross-subsidization went on back in time. Well, that disappeared by regulatory fiat. I mean you are not allowed to really try to do that anymore with our integrated market of investment banking, research, and trading.

Today, the question is, would dealers be incentivized to make that much of a difference in stocks that don't have enough natural liquidity to trade? The answer is no.[22] A varied menu should be offered or allowed.

In this regard, here are three things that have been talked about on this panel, and each of them could be enhanced. One is auctions. We are all familiar with

utilized fractions in price quotes. Since decimalization, all quotes appear in the decimal trading format." Source: Investopedia.

Read more: Decimal Trading https://www.investopedia.com/terms/d/decimal-trading.asp#ixzz56MmIr0Vz

Follow us: Investopedia on Facebook.

[19]The SEC's Order Handling Rules of 1997 and Beyond: Perspective and Outcomes of the Landmark Regulation RICHARD LINDSEY, JOHN AIDAN BYRNE, AND ROBERT A. SCHWARTZ. The Journal of Portfolio Management. Spring 2016 http://www.iijournals.com/doi/pdfplus/10.3905/jpm.2016.42.3.056.

[20]Jack Grubman was a former managing director at Salomon Smith Barney and lead research analyst for the telecommunications sector. (Smith Barney was a predecessor firm of Travelers' Salomon Smith Barney created in 1997. The following year, Salomon Smith Barney became part of Citigroup with the merger of Travelers and Citicorp.) In 2003, Grubman was banned by the SEC from the securities industry for life for allegedly disseminating misleading research. He paid fines of $15 million.

"It was at Salomon that he perfected the art of playing both sides of the Street; analyzing stocks for the investing public, while helping Salomon raise money or advise on mergers for the same companies he tracked."

Janey Guyon. *CNN Money.* May 16, 2005.

[21]Investment Banks and IPOs: Selecting a Bookrunner

Caleb Christensen May 24, 2018. IPOhub

https://www.ipohub.org/investment-banks-ipos-selecting-bookrunner/

[22]Weisberger is referring to that face that market makers don't want to make markets in thinly traded stocks, because there is no commercial upside if there is no volume. Taking risk and committing capital by way of two-sided quotes, and pushing the quote spread closer together makes economic sense only when there is a lot of volume, argue analysts. That's when the "micro alpha" trading extracts adds up to something worthwhile say, for example, gains of a fraction of a basis point, multiplied 500 thousand times. On stocks with small floats and not much liquidity, those tiny increments of price movement don't add up to enough "alpha" to be worth the transaction costs or the risk for traders.

single-price auctions, back when Steve Wunsch first started explaining this and pioneering the concept.[23] Jim Ross is too modest to market his own firm here today. But let me say his company is talking about doing block auctions and trying to collect liquidity in an intelligent manner! That is something that the market structure should facilitate. The second thing that should be enhanced is dealer markets. There are dealers who have an ax and who want to be the investment banker in a stock.[24] They can't profitably commit capital anymore, so that should be incentivized. That doesn't mean it's going to solve everything. It doesn't mean you want to beat the whole thing.

The other problem we have are agency algorithms, or algos, which are hamstrung, and have been for years. And this doesn't really impress people enough. For the most part, when you send 100 orders in a name to the firm you think will have the best ax in the stock, the firm that will be trading the most in the stock, you don't get 100 orders being managed by one algo trading the difference between the buys and the sells. You actually get 100 different algos! That's an enormous problem.

The reality is we've taken a market structure where a huge share of the order flow once went to the New York Stock Exchange, to the exchange specialists, who would see all these multiple orders and would choose how much money to make on each order. By the law of monopoly probably, the specialist would make more back then compared to today with all the rules and changes now in market structure.[25] But if we recognize that algos can be regulated— and I think we all realize that now—maybe they should be able to trade them altogether.[26] If you do that, that concentration in individual stocks would also be helpful. None of these are magic bullets. Yet all three kinds of make sense, I believe.

ROSS: We're talking about the small-cap stocks, right? There is obviously a lower shareholder base there. There's no question the small-cap stock is a more vulnerable stock. They're more vulnerable and more risky. There's those obvious elements. But that said, we should have a market structure and a market model that

[23] Founder of the now defunct Arizona Stock Exchange, an electronic stock exchange. A former Kidder Peabody vice president, the late Steve Wunsch was also known for his deep knowledge of market structure and for his passionate defense of free enterprise markets.

[24] Definition of Ax. Source Investopedia. https://www.investopedia.com/terms/a/ax.asp

[25] Weisberger is referring to the fact that the New York Stock Exchange once had a dominant and "monopolistic" share of trading in its own stocks.

[26] It is worth noting that because algorithms, by nature, break orders up into smaller "child" orders and are routed to venues that have demonstrated the best peformance against specific names or situations, this results in "market impact." This market impact occurs because every one of those small orders interacts with a slew of other small orders—and each execution gets printed to the tape, and therefore, the NBBO is moved bit by bit. "Physically not know about each other" may well be a reference to information leakage—these multiple executions are signalling the market that there is a lot of activity—which pushes the price away from a trading participant.

There has been significant discussion about requiring that every algo be "registered" with FINRA/SEC to provide data on how it is configured, how it works and "certifies" that it is seeking best execution on the client's behalf. Algo "certificiation" requirements are also raised under MiFID II.

allows for liquidity aggregation and price discovery in a way that helps get these kinds of stocks traded.

There are 23,400,000 milliseconds in a trading day.[27] We talk about fragmentation on the spatial side, which is where we can see the reality of the markets all doing the same thing, forcing investors to splinter their order shares across many markets. And that results in significant execution delay and missed trades. As costly to investors as spatial fragmentation may be, temporal or time fragmentation is even more caustic to investors' returns and more problematic in today's continuous and high-frequency marketplace. Trading in microseconds—that's a millionth of a second—continuously results in marketable contra orders missing one another in mere microseconds. And there are plenty of microseconds in a regular trading day—23.4 billion to be exact—to generate hundreds of millions, if not billions of missed trades in a single trading day. So today's problem of spatial fragmentation caused by 50-plus marketplaces, in comparison to the massive effect of time on order execution, is a market structure yet to be solved.

But solutions like electronic call auctions are appearing in the marketplace, and the results are very promising. I'm sorry, but the real pernicious fragmentation is time; it is temporal. You can't link time. Once again, on the idea of aggregating diverse liquidity, why do we need to aggregate, to centralize that flow somehow? We need diverse liquidity. And that's why you do need market makers. You do need institutions; you need all the different types because you don't have a trade without the tension in that market.

Now we're starting to pull together some elements of what a market model might look like.[28] And that might be something like a call auction. Clearly, aggregating liquidity at a single point in time allows us to do both of those things. And we need to start thinking about how we map our market structure to the actual tendencies and dynamics of the stock, itself.

COULSON: For institutions, I see call auctions as being very interesting, especially since they happen when the institution gets to price their market impact at the end of the day.

Your average smaller public company is majority owned by individuals. These individuals like trading through online brokers. Trading in little bits, they like the ease of instant low-cost executions. They don't want to wait around and say, "Did I get filled?" Because they don't have a high market impact and their trades are quickly filled by market makers.

But you must look at who it is working for and at who is trading these securities today. In that regard, we've introduced what we call a Q score. It's a daily data file

---

[27] Jim Ross is talking about how, given how fast a trade occurs in sub-millisecond speed, there are tens of millions of chances to trade in a moment. Compounded with multiple markets trading the same securities, that is an exponential level of complexity when you are trying to aggregate liquidity on thinly traded stocks.

[28] James Ross said in a follow-up interview that his reference to "we're" in this sentence refers to the industry and regulators. "It could be CODA Markets too...as that is what we are doing!" he added.

that calculates, per stock, the 20-day average excess liquidity provided by market makers and agency brokers on our system. This quantifies historical excess liquidity, which is above their quoted size. It includes a percentage of fills, and an average size of fills, so you get an idea of historical liquidity above a broker-dealer's quoted size.

What's interesting is learning about who has good Q scores and what type of Q scores they have. This data lets liquidity providers build clout or brand equity for the participant. For large retail market makers, we find that they have strong Q scores in the names they are most active in.

Then there are the international arbitrageurs, such as the electronic trading firm Jane Street. These market makers have consistent trade size in many ADRS and foreign ordinaries. We also see liquidity in specific names pop up from tier 2 institutional brokers. They're working a lot of "not held" liquidity into the market, those places where they're not showing their whole hand, which again goes to the panel's discussion on transparency. In other words, it isn't always a good idea to show all your cards.

How can we get better data around liquidity? That is what we need to focus on with markets so that investors understand the best strategy for each trade and how to find the right liquidity provider. If you're trading 200 shares, there's lots of choices. But if size goes up, you may have to work your order to get your trade complete. This is because most of the market volumes are from quickly executing smaller trades.

ROSS: But there is leakage, and that scares the crap out of an institution. Because you're saying, well, they will move the market, that's exactly what they're trying to avoid. The idea of letting people know, this is the tail or residual on the order, so I'm done. For example, say you had 10,000 shares to trade, and you end up trading 500 shares satisfactorily. But now you still have to trade 9500, and that tail or residual gets whipped around a bit. When you don't reveal you have a tail on an order, market participants will be thinking, "Well, there's more to come!" They are either going to get on board or avoid such a trade. The issue gets back to this: We don't have a market model that really serves the needs of covering leakage and the impact that occurs in our continuous market.

COULSON: When there is a seller in the market, the smart buyer will try to test the seller's lower limits, to ultimately buy at the best prices. Buyers want to get filled at the lowest price.

WEISBERGER: Look, there's a fundamental tension in market structure between price discovery and transaction costs that doesn't get talked about enough. If you're an exchange, you talk about price discovery as the only thing that matters, and if you're an institutional broker, you talk about minimizing transaction costs, which is the only thing that matters. The reality is that both matter. Institutions care about it, if they know, if the world knows, that someone is trying to buy 10 percent of a company. The price would immediately jump up, the institution would get nothing bought, and then they'd be starting at a higher level.[29] They obviously consider that

[29] When a market participant's intention to make a major move in a stock is readily discernible, the price moves away from them (moving up when trying to buy and down when trying to sell). That drives up the participant's cost basis for that trade and makes performance more challenging.

bad. But if you're an academic and you want to know price discovery, well, that's price discovery. And what Jim is basically saying is that the institutions should be able to minimize transaction costs because it's what they are trying to do.

I think it goes back to workflow. At the end of the day, if you're an institution, you are trying to outperform a benchmark. People were talking about stock picking. Let's face it, the other big issue with small- and mid-cap liquidity is passive investing. And the reason is simple. If you want to buy a stock that is not in your benchmark, you had better—excuse me, I can't say the word I was going to use—well, be right because otherwise, you've just institutionalized underperformance.

Think about what that means. The Russell 2000 is a common benchmark, but a lot of people are benchmarked to the S&P. But even with the Russell 2000, for any stocks that fall underneath that threshold, they might as well not exist, which means if you buy them—and, by the way, that's why they're 80 percent individuals—you have to be a specialty fund, or you have to be part of someone's asset allocation.[30] As an aside, in those index funds, all the pricing happens at the close.[31]

So now you're a portfolio manager, you're trying to beat your benchmark, and you've done your homework overnight. You have your idea of where things are, and everything that moves in pricing from the open to the close is blind to you—unless you change your workflow to essentially choose your price, you know, whatever, 20 minutes before the close, and say I'm going to participate in the closing auction on what I want to buy. And if I don't get it, I don't care. Well, what does it mean to say that if you don't get it, you don't care? The truth is they could buy index funds to make up the difference so they're not out of the market.[32] But a lot of portfolio managers don't think that way. So active versus passive becomes a big reason why small-caps have a problem, because institutions find it difficult to navigate that outperformance.[33]

SCHACK: I want to focus next on how to make things better. We haven't talked in any detail about the tick pilot, as loath as I am to bring that up again.[34] We've been trading under it for a little while now. Has it helped, or will it help?

---

[30] David Weisberger's point is this: You won't get access to this liquidity necessarily on the open market because it is too hard to find.

[31] This is referring to the concentration of liquidity/high volume of trading at the close.

[32] Weisberger is referring to why small-caps are so thinly traded, underbought, and sold. This is essentially the culmination of the case he has been building in his comments on this panel: Small-cap and thinly traded stocks don't get attention from market makers because there is no commercial upside or incentive. They trade in very small lot sizes, cause much impact, and are more volatile than large caps. They are left out of the trend toward Index or ETF investing because they don't make the threshold of the benchmarks that usually drive those instruments.

Generally, Weisberger's thesis seems to be that today's market structure and the motivations of its participants disadvantage the entire class of small-cap stocks.

[33] This comment relates to portfolio managers' goals for participating in the stories of small-cap stocks: They are hard to buy, liquidity is thin, and there is lots of potential negative selection if you try to buy cash equity.

[34] Referring to pilot program for trading small-cap stocks in wider minimum increments. See SEC Approves Pilot Program to Assess Tick Size Impact for Smaller Companies. Center for Financial Stability, May 7, 2015. http://centerforfinancialstability.org/wp/?p=5987

FIRMIN: I feel like I've been in the middle of a big sort of domestic argument here.

SCHACK: Auctions versus dealers, fight night!

FIRMIN: Is the tick pilot working?[35] No is the short answer. I mean, we've got enough information now out of the couple of weeks of group one and two.[36] There were a broad range of objectives set out for what the tick pilot was going to achieve. Some of them were pretty grand, centered around sort of generating jobs and improving transparency.

By looking at the group one and two names as they've been trading so far, what we've seen is almost the exact opposite of what was intended. You've seen quotes widen but that's because the majority of these stocks now have their spreads constrained by these nickel tick sizes. So you get a natural increase in quote spreads because of increased competition from the likes of quant guys who are building up. Is it real liquidity? Probably not.

Have you seen a material change in volumes, because that was the other objective? No, it's still just noise.[37] I mean there's an argument to be made that it's still early in the process and we should wait a little bit longer. But there is something particularly pronounced. What is pronounced, even at this early stage, is the venue types that are making up the trading in these names now.

What you have seen for group one and group two is traditional maker-taker style venues lose like 10 percent of their market share in these names. And here's who they have lost it to: They lost it to inverted venues where people try and jump the queue, so 6 percent or so of that 10 percent is going to inverted venues, and the rest is going into TRF venues.[38] With the intention of trying to promote liquidity trading, it's actually had the opposite effect. You've increased a lot of the stuff that is going on in the dark.

SCHACK: Any divergent views from anybody else?

ROSS: Well, I'm not surprised. There was something intriguing about the tick pilot, and that is the concept of widening spreads. This idea that maybe there is more liquidity outside the NBBO. Decimalization and rebates collapsed spreads, thus making liquidity discovery more difficult. Maybe there's a way to generate liquidity outside the spread. The tick pilot was about compensating market makers, not about unleashing institutional liquidity held away from the market. The point here is that

---

[35] See footnote 17.

[36] Firmin is referring to the sample groups of the pilot.

[37] By "noise," he means quote traffic by market makers or quants who are pinging multiple pools to find the natural midpoint (and who will trade out and be net zero by close), but not by fundamental investors who are buying and holding.

[38] As noted by one trading executive, traders use "inverted venues to 'cut the queue' because cost-sensitive smart order routers target inverted venues first." As he further elaborated, to trade passively in stocks with large queues at the primary exchange, "the only way to do so is by posting on a different exchange."

TRF is the acronym for Trade Reporting Facility, the place where off-exchange trades are reported.

there is meaningful and viable liquidity out there. But, currently, decimalization and rebates tend to collapse the spread. And, with tight ticks, there is no chance of that liquidity ever being found. Maybe we've overly compressed spreads in the mid- and the small-cap stocks, the micro-cap stocks. Maybe we've had an adverse effect in general compared with the intentions of the tick-size program. But, to be fair, there is not a lot of that rebate stuff going on in the small caps, and I know that.

Let's just say, for a minute, that the NBBOs are overly compressed in these stocks, so dealers have to take more risk with less profit opportunity. What the tick pilot was envisioning with mandates—that is to say wider spreads—is that by increasing tick sizes, dealers would have greater profit opportunity to offset their risk and would be more willing to provide liquidity to less liquid securities. The issue that I have is, first of all, that the uniform mandating of tick sizes across a group of stocks ignores the uniqueness and idiosyncrasies of each individual stock, and any regulatory mandate on tick size is simply making matters worse for investors and issuers in the form of transaction costs. There is little assurance of increased liquidity. In the end, no matter what the tick sizes and the regulatory mandates to support their business models, dealers can effectively only provide liquidity to a multitrillion-dollar equity market.

The dealer-centric market was fine in the nineteenth and twentieth centuries but, today, it is just outdated and fails to meet the needs of today's retail and institutional investors. The only real solution is for our market structure to develop more effective ways for retail and institutional investors to interact with one another. Therefore, rather than focusing on dealer profits and tick sizes, our markets need to address spatial/temporal fragmentation, adverse selection, information leakage, and market impact. These are the issues that really hurt trade quality and investor performance.

I don't like the idea of mandating tick sizes. In fact, it is the likes of market participants with the use of limit orders and so on who should be driving price discovery as opposed to regulators mandating pricing rules.[39]

FIRMIN: Sorry, you're not fixing spreads; you're fixing the tick size.[40]

ROSS: The tick size, yes, the tick size.

FIRMIN: But there's a massive difference there.

ROSS: Okay.

FIRMIN: There is a massive difference there. And I think this is one of the most underappreciated things about US market structure in terms of that penny tick. That penny tick means something very different if you're a SIRI versus an Amazon at $800.[41] And it changes completely the economics of how those stocks are going to trade. What point is there in trying to manage passive liquidity provision when it costs .13 basis points for someone to trade a stock priced at $6.00?

[39] An analysis of the pilot: https://www.sec.gov/dera/staff-papers/white-papers/dera_wp_tick_size-market_quality

[40] See footnote 17.

[41] Stock symbol for Sirius XM Radio.

You see the whole liquidity landscape changes with liquidity moving away from maker-taker venues to the inverted pools to compensate for the smaller spreads. [42] And, at some point, the economics just breaks down, and all the liquidity providers have just gone out. And at that point, rather than having this sort of nice, linear relationship between tick sizes and effective spreads, all the spreads blow up. That becomes a real cost for people who are trading these names. And at the other end of the spectrum that you are talking about, you've got a situation where the tick size is just too big. And for penny stocks, it's Reg NMS enforced.[43] But that's where you see this competition that we're talking about. You see the sort of HFT guys (again, an overlapping term perhaps), but you see them come in and you see the thicker quotes. You see a migration of flow to inverse venues as people try to queue jump.[44] And it's a very, very different landscape. Each of those ends of that spectrum is a material cost that I think is quite underappreciated.

SCHACK: Switching gears, let's consider the idea of let's not have a one-size-fits-all market structure. It's being put forward that you should have one exchange for some of these stocks. If you happen to be the listing market on a new emerging growth company or something, then you should have an exclusive listing for some period of time before it becomes multiple listed. Would something like that help?

COULSON: Exclusive listings are a monopoly, which is nice if it's your exchange and frustrating if you are a broker forced to use that one exchange. I think it is unbelievable that regulators are still considering granting trading monopolies. We should provide more competition, not less.

The second piece is that the exchange listing process is broken for small public companies. An IPO task force showed that it costs around a million and a half dollars a year to be listed on an exchange. That is what's stopping companies from wanting to become public. The regulatory burden on public companies needs to be addressed.

It's too costly and too time-consuming to be public. If we really want to focus on how we change these things, let's look again at what the Internet has done. Every

[42] David Firmin was saying that liquidity moved away from maker-taker venues to the inverted pools to compensate for the smaller spreads. See attached white paper for an explanation:

https://papers.ssrn.com/sol3/papers.cfm?abstract_id=2939012

In a competitive program to encourage trading on exchanges, maker-taker fees offer a transaction rebate to trading participants who provide liquidity, charging customers who take liquidity.

Read more: What Maker-Taker Fees Mean To You | Investopedia http://www.investopedia.com/articles/active-trading/042414/what-makertaker-fees-mean-you.asp#ixzz4IvzckkIR

Follow us: Investopedia on Facebook.

[43] The SEC introduced Rule 612—or the Sub-Penny Rule—in 2005 to address these issues. In particular, the rule states that the minimum price increments for stocks over $1.00 must be $0.01, and stocks under $1.00 can increment by $0.0001.

https://www.sec.gov/divisions/marketreg/subpenny612faq.htm#q13

[44] Queue jumping occurs when a market participant tries to jump ahead of other orders lined up at a certain price point. See more: http://market-microstructure.institutlouisbachelier.org/uploads/91_7%20MOALLEMI%202014-12-paris-mm-queue-value.pdf

Internet business model is about being a service for providing the information so that the user can make better choices. That's how you lower the cost of being public. You opt for the Wikipedia model. In other words, you put more information out there, and you let investors make informed choices.

In discussing venture markets, we should focus on two things: How do we lower listing costs? And how do we lower the cost of raising capital? Those are the real problems to solve.

When we talk to community banks that are leaving the exchanges, they tell us it is "too much time, too much complexity, and too much cost."

SCHACK: Well, we'll have to conclude on that interesting note from Cromwell. We have lots to think and talk about for the next conference.

Thank you so much, gentlemen.

Chapter 5
New Approaches for Creating Liquidity

Robert A. Schwartz, Ian Domowitz, Robert Barnes, William Dove, Amy Edwards, Robert Schwartz, and Greg Wojciechowski

IAN DOMOWITZ: This panel will discuss new approaches to liquidity. New approaches is probably a good term. Simply put, the single negative thing one can mention about some of the views expressed today is this: There's a bit of revisionist history involved. Fortunately, the advantage of being just a little bit older than others in the room is my memory tells me the specialist system didn't solve everything in the past. In fact, the market makers ended up colluding, and flash crashes started not in May of 2010 but rather back in 1962.[1] Given the market size back in 1962, it was

[1] The Flash Crash of 1962, Barry Ritholtz. May 29, 2010 https://ritholtz.com/2010/05/the-flash-crash-of-1962/

Flash Crash of May 6, 2010, lasted about 36 minutes, erasing 998.5 points in the Dow Jones Industrial Average and then quickly recouped much of the losses as the various indexes rapidly rebounded in this high-speed, electronic trading phenomena.

R. A. Schwartz (✉)
Zicklin School of Business, Baruch College - CUNY, New York, NY, USA
e-mail: robert.schwartz@baruch.cuny.edu

I. Domowitz
Managing Director, CEO, ITG Solutions Network, New York, NY, USA

R. Barnes
Turquoise, LSEG, London, UK

W. Dove
Extraordinary RE, Princeton, NJ, USA

A. Edwards
US Securities & Exchange Commission, Washington, DC, USA

R. Schwartz
Zicklin School of Business, Baruch College - CUNY, New York, NY, USA

G. Wojciechowski
The Bermuda Stock Exchange, Pembroke, Bermuda

R. A. Schwartz et al. (eds.), *Liquidity*, Zicklin School of Business Financial Markets Series, https://doi.org/10.1007/978-3-031-36914-8_5

actually much worse than the more recent one that everybody talks about. In 1962, it was a case of where the specialists all went the wrong way. The specialists didn't get out; they literally traded against.[2] This was a scandal at the time. And, by the way, it took a year to get a report written on the events of 1962. I guess it also took a year to do a report for the flash crash of 2010.[3] I'm not sure how much progress we have made since the events of 1962.

It is now the day after Halloween. Creating liquidity does sound a bit like alchemy, the turning of lead into gold! The one thing you should know about me as your moderator is this. I'm one of those people who does not believe that liquidity is volume. I believe that liquidity is abstract enough that you can't talk about it without talking about price.

That is another feature of this conference. I mean that relative to even last year, the year before, and certainly the last 5 years, I've started to hear talk about the fact that there is a price to liquidity. We teach our freshman in this university that you can't have supply and demand without talking about prices. Liquidity is basically the same thing.

I want to start with some kind of definition. Amy Edwards, from the regulator's point of view, really the academic point of view in your case, let's try to define this a little bit for the sake of conversation.

AMY EDWARDS: I am from the Securities and Exchange Commission. As such, I have to say I speak on my own behalf, and not on behalf of Mike Piwowar, or any of the other commissioners, or any other staff members. When I'm providing a definition of liquidity, it is my own.

I see liquidity as being multifaceted. It is the ability to trade when you want, the amount that you want, when you want, and at the price you want. There are many facets to it. There's a time dimension, a price dimension, and a size dimension.

DOMOWITZ: Bob, you've already been quoted! I'm going to give you the floor shortly with respect to your definition that came up just an hour ago.

ROBERT SCHWARTZ: Amy just hit the three points that I'd want to hit. It's when do you want to trade, can you trade fast enough, can you trade in sufficient size, and can you trade at a reasonably good price. How do you implement something like that? Well, there's a counterpart to what I've long heard the exchanges and the New York Stock Exchange say, and that is depth, breadth, and resiliency. Depth and breadth are the size, and if you have it on the book, you can trade quickly.

How about resiliency? Am I correct in saying that's kind of a relatively new focus in the academic literature? It's definitely there now. I would characterize it by adding a few more words about it. Depth and breadth are static liquidity. It's what's

---

[2] In a follow-up, Ian Domowitz asserted that back in 1962, when this aforementioned flash crash occurred, the specialists were not fulfilling their historical role as liquidity providers (of last resort), trading against, and going the wrong way, to use his own description. "It was a bit of a scandal back then," he added.

[3] Referring to a regulatory review.

on the book. Resiliency? Maybe, Ian, you can ask me to define it in a subsequent question.

DOMOWITZ: No, it's not so new. I think I put the title with resiliency on it back in 2001.

SCHWARTZ: Yes, but what's new about it is my definition. Resiliency is a dynamic dimension. As a dynamic dimension, it refers to price. Is it a good price? Now I'll tell you another word for resiliency. It isn't a definition, but it's the other side of the coin. It's price discovery. It's very, very similar. I heard this on the previous panel. I also heard it in what you were saying. If you have a market where depth and breadth are good but price is all over the place, attention is called to price.

In my work, we measure resiliency as a dynamic component, and we are finding that companies that do not exhibit this resiliency, this ability to trade at more sharply discovered prices, have shares that are priced lower, and their cost of capital is raised.

DOMOWITZ: One of the traps we can fall into is this: We tend to be so equity focused in our talk about market structure. Today, we can have a break with that tradition. I'd like to ask you, Will, to speak to some of this, in particular with respect to the challenges of liquidity creation, if you will, in a market that people don't know so much about.

WILLIAM DOVE: I head a startup venture called Extraordinary RE.[4] Extraordinary RE is building the first trading platform for insurance liabilities. This will open up a new marketplace to allow insurance companies to transfer specific defined insurance risks to institutional investors. By creating such a market, this will enable insurers to access new types of capital for peak risks. It will also create a new low correlation asset class for institutional investors.

Anyone who is engaged in starting a new trading market encounters challenges. How do you attract investors and maintain liquidity? Extraordinary RE will face some unique challenges that are particular to the insurance liability asset class. Some examples are high levels of price volatility. There can be long periods of time where you don't have any new information emerging that will lead investors to adjust their expectations of intrinsic value. You'll have periods of heightened uncertainty during an emerging situation. For example, with a hurricane approaching Florida, everyone is watching *The Weather Channel*, or the NOAA website for the latest updates on the track.[5] That creates a lot of uncertainty. Even after an event like that, there can be a long period of time when a liability can be difficult to value even after it has occurred.

Extraordinary RE's approach to addressing the challenges is to implement a patented market design and the trading rules we've created to support liquidity in the context of these challenges. One of the most critical design elements—which I know is near and dear to Bob Schwartz's heart—is having a call auction trading

[4] Extraordinary RE. https://www.extraordinaryre.com/

[5] National Oceanic and Atmospheric Agency.

model. This will maximize the liquidity available, focusing it at the points in time when the auctions are called, which will be multiple times each trading day.

DOMOWITZ: That obviously is a departure from what we would think such a market would start from, which was sort of the OTC view of dealership. But it makes me also think that in a new asset class, you have some structural issues to deal with. We see that even in the equity markets. Greg, please speak to that. You actually had to start from scratch, so to speak, in terms of capital markets.

GREG WOJCIECHOWSKI: When he asked me to sit on this panel, I said, Bob [Schwartz], we just created a market in Bermuda.[6] But we don't have liquidity. What can we really add to that topic? One of the things I'm sensing has me wondering whether I should be optimistic or pessimistic about liquidity. I thought that way from the beginning as you design a market. In any event, I'll start with the things that are absolutely needed to create the platform to help develop an environment of liquidity.

I will add a different kind of piece to that. The theme of our talk today is how do you prepare for liquidity. In Bermuda, that's what we're doing right now. I would like to leave this conference today on a note of optimism, that when you prepare for liquidity the right way and you have all the pieces in place, you'll be able to get it, and you'll be able to achieve it. I'm hearing a lot of different discussions right now in this market about how to actually find it and how to capture it.

We're approaching it in a different way. In Bermuda, we're basically a textbook model. We started from the ground up, looking at the regulatory infrastructure, and at the technical infrastructure. We are also talking to market investors to get them ready in order to be able to provide liquidity. We're a bit unusual in the sense that we don't have the size or scope in terms of the country size or the market size compared to other markets. Therefore, we're going to look at liquidity a bit differently than many other markets will look at it. This will fit in with what Will is saying. We will look at creating liquidity in different places or in different asset classes.

We'll always have a requirement to provide everything you're talking about here to our domestic capital market in the context of an exchange structure. For a smaller exchange like ours supporting a smaller economy, it's not so much about finding liquidity but rather about helping to create the infrastructure that will support users in bringing products to market that will, in turn, create demand which could translate into new liquidity.

I won't apologize. I'm an exchange guy. We do what exchanges do. There is a lot of discussion about whether that's the right model or the wrong model. But as you're developing a capital market, or supporting a domestic capital market, a framework must be in place, one that will help guide things along.

There also must be, in my position as a CEO, some entrepreneurial spirit. What Will talks about is interesting, that is, exchanging and creating liquidity in new asset classes. In that regard, we're very focused on the outside of the traditional market. For instance, we're very focused on cat bond products, or catastrophe bonds as they

[6] Bermuda Stock Exchange. http://www.bsx.com/

are called.[7] We're looking at how to migrate those products from a dark market onto a more lit platform.[8]

After talking and listening to all of you today, I'm hopeful that I will walk away from here a little more optimistic that liquidity is something that we can actually obtain if we prepare for it in the right way.

DOMOWITZ: In an offline conversation, Greg and I talked about the exchange traded model, the contribution (or not) of the alternative trading systems. That was before I knew Robert Barnes was going to be on the panel. Since he's had his feet over time in both worlds—exchange trading and off-exchange trading—I'd like you to speak to that. You can talk about it in terms of liquidity provision. Greg's problem was, in a sense, free riding.[9] You might want to say something about that. And please give us your view on the role of the ATS structure within the exchange regulatory framework.[10]

ROBERT BARNES: The regulatory framework is one of the other frameworks that is important. We wish to thank the regulators because they provide this framework within which we can behave as entrepreneurs.

If I might just humbly share this observation about the different philosophies in the approach to regulation in the United States and the European markets. Simply put, under Reg NMS in the US, the rules prescribe how you handle your limit order in terms of routing to the various destinations.[11]

In Europe, however, it's completely the opposite. The regulatory obligation in Europe is to display the limit order, unless there is a pre-trade transparency waiver that allows the participant to place a firm order where the price and size is not

[7] A catastrophe bond (CAT) is a high-yield debt instrument that is designed to raise money for companies in the insurance industry in the event of a natural disaster. A CAT bond allows the issuer to receive funding from the bond only if specific conditions, such as an earthquake or tornado, occur. If an event protected by the bond activates a payout to the insurance company, the obligation to pay interest and repay the principal is either deferred or completely forgiven. Source: Investopedia

[8] See, related for a comprehensive account of dark pools and there opposite in lit markets, Dark Pools: Fear of the Dark. Third Way. Lauren Oppenheimer, John Vahey. August 28, 2013. http://www.thirdway.org/report/dark-pools-fear-of-the-dark

As the authors explain: "Dark pools are private, electronic stock trading venues that allow buyers and sellers of a stock to be matched anonymously. In a dark pool, prices are not displayed to investors—stock prices are dark. Dark trading is an alternative to trading on a "lit" exchange, like the New York Stock Exchange (NYSE), where traders benefit from visible prices."

[9] This refers to taking advantage of something that others pay for without paying

[10] Alternative Trading Systems (ATS). *Investopedia.* James Chen. April 18, 2019. https://www.investopedia.com/terms/a/alternative-trading-system.asp Systems.

[11] In the United States, Reg NMS (Regulation National Market System) was adopted by the Securities and Exchange Commission in 2005 and introduced 2 years later to further advance the ideals of a national market system. The regulation includes the order protection or trade-through rule, access rule (fair access) to market data including quotations, and rules on sub-penny trading and on market data.

displayed pre-trade.[12] But post-trade everything must be revealed in real time so that post-trade transparency becomes like pre-trade transparency for the next trade.

The next observation—and why the regulatory authorities play such an important role—is this: In Europe, there was a famous report in 2001 called the Wise Men Report.[13] The report articulated that the demographics of developed countries are growing old, people are living longer, which is a good thing. But, of course, governments can no longer afford old age social security. Therefore, that raised the issue of privatizing pensions through the financial markets, and it put a focus on encouraging direct contributions to pensions as a mechanism for long-term financial health. Yet, at that time, the humble observation was that assets were growing much faster in the US than they were in Europe, partly due to the costs of trading, clearing, and settlement across borders. And Rainer Riess gave a very nice summary today about how the European markets have evolved.[14]

Here's what we have seen as a market operator. We heard about the 30th anniversary of the Big Bang in London from open outcry to computers.[15] This month is the 10th anniversary of Turquoise as a concept that originated back in 2016.[16] That is when we initiated Project Turquoise to create a single-order book, on a venue called Turquoise, to trade all of the European single market securities from large-caps to small-caps, and in advance of MiFID.[17]

But it was also introduced to innovate some form of smart, anonymous block auctioning. I'm very pleased to say that last year, 2015, year nine of the platform's introduction, was the first year that Turquoise processed over one trillion euros of turnover on an order book from 19 countries. That encompassed not just the developed, but also the emerging markets.

Turquoise also launched an innovation by utilizing the same connections and servers as our users and customers into the London data center that accesses the London Stock Exchange in Turquoise. That was accomplished through STP, or straight-through processing. There is another regulatory framework coming in MiFID II, known as Double Volume Caps. This will mean a constraint on the dark pools, particularly for certain order sizes impacted by the DVC.[18]

---

[12] See MiFID 11. Pre- and post-trade transparency. Hogan Lovells. January 2016. https://www.hoganlovells.com/~/media/hogan-lovells/pdf/mifid/subtopic-pdf/lwdlib01-4923975-v1-mifid_ii_transparency_jan_2016_v2.pdf

[13] See BEST EXECUTION, April 17, 2019. Interview with Dr. Robert Barnes. https://www.bestexecution.net/equities-trading-focus-turquoise/

[14] See Chapter 3, Opening Address: Liquidity in the European Experience

[15] How the Big Bang changed the City of London forever. Jamie Robertson Business reporter, BBC News. 26 October 2016. https://www.bbc.com/news/business-37751599?ocid=socialflow_twitter&

[16] Turquoise. https://www.londonstockexchange.com/trade/turquoise-markets-and-instruments

[17] Markets in Financial Instruments Directive I, or MiFID I, introduced in October 2010, was followed by the second MiFID proposals, or MiFID II, in September 2012, aiming for the reform and harmonization of European area markets. MiFID II shifts the European regulatory regime from a principles-based to a more US-style, rules-based regulatory model.

[18] DVC is a major innovation MiFID II applied to all equity instruments.

The objective of the double volume cap is to limit the execution of transactions in dark pools.

What does DVC mean for investors? For investors who choose to trade at the midpoint for potential price improvement, orders below a certain scale probably won't be allowed to do that. These investors won't be able to get that potential price improvement unless the order received by the market operator is of a certain large scale so it is not crimped by the DVC. What does this then boil down to?

Two significant trends that are particularly relevant in Europe and are also going global are worth noting. One is the growth in passive indexation and passive investment, which we heard about on the earlier panels. Second, increasingly, the asset owners on the buy-side want to outperform benchmarks by trading electronic blocks.

I will conclude by saying that we've been very pleased to see that, with the support of customers, we've been able to design a market mechanism that is a large in scale electronic execution channel that works.

DOMOWITZ: Speaking of MiFID, we've had a lot of activity in the US. The tick pilot's already on the table at this conference.[19] I'd like to call on Amy again in terms of current initiatives that are actually focused on liquidity. What should we make of that? Is there a takeaway from your perspective?

EDWARDS: There are several initiatives. Some of them are SRO focused, and some are commission focused. I'd start with some issuer pay type of initiatives.[20] Europe has had issuer pay for a while. That is where the issuer pays for market

---

The double volume cap deals with two types of transactions benefiting from a waiver:

1. Transactions that are executed in systems where the price is determined by reference to a price generated by another system (reference price waiver)
2. Transactions that are bilaterally negotiated and formalized on a trading venue (negotiated transaction waiver).

The double volume cap limits the transactions that can be executed under both those waivers at 4% at a trading venue level and at 8% for all EU trading venues.

https://www.emissions-euets.com/internal-electricity-market-glossary/2021-double-volume-cap-transparency-regime-under-mifid-iiSource: Double volume cap (DVC) transparency regime under MiFID II.

Source: Glowacki Law Firm.

See DOUBLE VOLUME CAP MECHANISM.

https://www.esma.europa.eu/double-volume-cap-mechanism#:~:text=The%20double%20volume%20cap%20mechanism%20%28DVCM%29%20%28Article%205,%28b%29%20%28i%29%20of%20MiFIR%29%20in%20an%20equity%20instrument

[19] Referring to pilot program for trading small-cap stocks in wider minimum increments. See SEC Approves Pilot Program to Assess Tick Size Impact for Smaller Companies. Center for Financial Stability, May 7, 2015. http://centerforfinancialstability.org/wp/?p=5987

Press Release. Securities and Exchange Commission. May 6, 2015. https://www.sec.gov/news/pressrelease/2015-82.html

[20] SRO is the acronym for Self-Regulatory Organization.

Proposals, for example, featured payments by investors or by some external agency that could be the government, regulators, or stock exchanges.

See Issuers-Pays models ensures ratings are available to the entire market. The Economic Times. May 06, 2010.

https://m.economictimes.com/issuer-pays-model-ensures-ratings-are-available-to-the-entire-market/articleshow/5896079.cms

making services to help subsidize market makers. In the US, we have three programs run by Bats, Arca, and NASDAQ that operate only in the ETF or ETP space at the moment.[21] We've seen some interest over the last few years. But there is not a lot of interest by ETPs being in these programs. And the SROs are producing some empirical analyses, and at this point, we haven't seen any strong evidence.[22]

The most compelling thing seems to be that when an ETP is on one exchange, it draws liquidity from another exchange. But there's not a lot of evidence that it is increasing overall liquidity. There is also an initiative by the NYSE to create a mid-day auction in small- and mid-cap securities. I haven't seen any empirical analysis on that. I haven't heard much about how that is working. But I note that Europe has some of these midday auctions as well. They are very popular when they launch. But you don't really hear a lot about whether they're successful afterwards. I haven't seen any empirical analysis on that either.

As you know, within limit up/limit down, one of the main reasons to have limit up/limit down is to take care of temporary liquidity gaps.[23] One of the big results that was very evident on August 24 is that there were signs prior to August 24 of a lack of interest in the reopening auctions.[24] The Equity Market Structure Advisory Committee, particularly the Subcommittee on Market Quality, has been looking at that in particular, trying to figure out if there is a solution to improve the liquidity of the reopening auctions.[25] Also, the SROs in the context of the NMS plan, and also in their own roles, have been trying to figure out how to fix these auctions.[26]

DOMOWITZ: I was very interested in what David Firmin of Instinet had to say earlier today at this conference about the tick pilot results so far.[27] We track it, too, so let me give you an idea. Our observations are basically confirmatory of his statements.

As you aggregate up from a penny to a nickel—and I say aggregate because I think that's what's going on—you are seeing two to three times the available offering, at the best bid and offer. That's the good news.

---

[21] ETP is the acronym for Exchange Traded Product.

[22] https://www.sec.gov/files/rules/sro/nscc-an/2015/34-75730.pdf

[23] See NASDAQ Frequently Asked Questions: https://www.nasdaqtrader.com/content/MarketRegulation/LULD_FAQ.pdf

[24] August 24, 2015, is etched on many traders' memories. The S&P 500 opened at 1965.15 and within minutes fell to a low of 1867.01, a 5 percent decline. Intraday, the market gained back most of the loss, but toward the close of trading stocks fell again, ending the day 3.66 percent below the open.

If a market is forced to pause due to regulatory or other requirements, it needs of course to be reopened. An auction may be used for that purpose.

[25] Referring to the SEC Committee and Sub-committee. See Memorandum. Recommendations for Rulemaking on Issues of Market Quality. July 25, 2016

https://www.sec.gov/spotlight/emsac/emsac-market-quality-subcommittee-recomendation-072516.pdf

[26] As of writing in late 2021, the NMS review was underway.

[27] See NYSE Tick Pilot FAQs

https://www.nyse.com/tick-pilot/faqs

The bad news is trade volume is down, anywhere between 17 and 18 percent on average.[28] We're not seeing any good reason for that right now, so it's speculation. Certainly, I mean that's not just an averaging; roughly 75 percent of the 197 stocks that are currently trading under the tick pilot have been in so-called groups one and two.[29] Those of you who follow this have seen the volumes decline rather radically.

On the market structure point, I think Mr. Firmin said it was all going kind of from maker-taker to taker-maker.[30] I haven't looked at that. But I can tell you that dark trading has increased by roughly five percentage points in the small- and mid-caps that are subject to this regulation, going up from roughly 37 percent to 42 percent in terms of execution.[31]

That should be very intuitive to some of you since these dark pools are basically splitting the difference on the quote.[32] The difference has gotten bigger, and the savings are greater.[33] But I would say that that sort of destroys the argument that you will get a more transparent liquid market.

Now, the dark pools, given the way they operate, were once periodic.[34] I want to return to the issue of auctions and a transition from OTC.[35] I'd actually like to go back to Will on this. This is for both you and Bob Schwartz. No one doubts the theoretical superiority of the call auction. I mean, by and large, that's been well established. The problem has always been implementation, as opposed to the mechanics, or the benefits.[36] That is a liquidity discussion. But it has a temporal component, the

---

[28] According to an ITG report

[29] The tick pilot was divided into four groups of stocks, and each of the four groups was monitored separately.

[30] In a competitive program to encourage trading on exchanges, maker-taker fees offer a transaction rebate to trading participants who provide liquidity, charging customers who take liquidity.

Read more: What Maker-Taker Fees Mean To You | Investopedia http://www.investopedia.com/articles/active-trading/042414/what-makertaker-fees-mean-you.asp#ixzz4IvzckkIR

Follow us: Investopedia on Facebook.

By the same token, consider an inverted venue for an understanding of taker-maker:

An inverted venue refers to an exchange that offers two models to lure more equity trading volume, the conventional maker-taker model and a taker-maker model, or inverted rebate system where the liquidity taker is paid for handling a trade. Examples of exchanges offering inverted rebates have included Nasdaq BX, Bats BYX, and Bats EDGA.

[31] See NYSE Tick Pilot FAQs.

https://www.nyse.com/tick-pilot/faqs

Citing ITG research

[32] If two parties trade at the midpoint as is the norm in a dark pool, then each party saves one-half of the spread compared to hitting the bid or lifting the offer.

[33] Bigger spread implies that half the new spread is bigger than the old half.

[34] Periodic as in "periodic auctions" as noted in research by Professor Robert Schwartz.

[35] Referring to the transition from over the counter to auction markets.

[36] Referring to the idea of implementing a solid theoretical construct into an operating product or platform.

so-called pari-mutuel problem leading up to such an auction.[37] How is that being dealt with in an area that we don't even know about at this point?

DOVE: As far as dealing with time?

DOMOWITZ: Absolutely.

DOVE: Our marketplace would operate, with initially four auctions, ramping up to six and then to eight auctions per trading day. Another part of our design is to track the actual trading of each issue that we listed on the platform. We don't expect that every issue will trade at every auction. But we do need to maintain some level of price discovery so that if there is a period of time when an issue doesn't trade for multiple auctions or several days, we need to be able to force some small trades to generate price discovery. We'll inform the marketplace and then, in most cases, institute more voluntary trading.

DOMOWITZ: That's the liquidity component. Bob, we've spoken about it a couple of times. But in terms of the implementation, I am interested in your thoughts on the problems that have plagued us in the US. In other words, leading up to the auction, all the experiments with trying to price that and so forth. Fundamentally, this so-called pari-mutuel problem has really plagued the implementation of call auctions.[38] In this country, anyway. Do you have thoughts as to how that might be improved? Call auction is what it is, right?

SCHWARTZ: Thank you for the question and for giving me the title of my next paper, which is "The Theoretical Superiority of a Call Auction."

I go way back on a call auction. For one thing, I was involved in AZX.[39]

AZX was ahead of its time and too far out in front of the pack. There are a couple of problems with a call. One, I would always say from an academic point of view, is that it isn't sufficiently understood. For another thing, it is a gaming sort of strategy; it's very difficult to get the book to build, especially at the opening call. I co-authored a paper in the *Journal of Financial Markets* on the subject.[40] Finally, if all the market participants are there to participate in the call, the results for them are better than when fewer show up. But they don't all show up.

---

[37] Pari-Mutuel Systems and Knightian Uncertainty. Here are two mental models that explain the nature of the stock market. By Oliver Sung

https://junto.investments/stock-market-models/#:~:text=A%20pari-mutuel%20system%20is%20one%20in%20which%20all,words%2C%20the%20odds%20change%20based%20on%20what%E2%80%99s%20bet

[38] See Guide to Para-Mutual Betting https://www.gamblingsites.com/sports-betting/types/pari-mutuel/

Source: Gamblingsites.com

[39] AZX, or The Arizona Stock Exchange, was an electronic stock exchange founded in 1990 as Wunsch Auction Systems by R. Steven Wunsch. AZX moved from New York City to Arizona in 1992 and was then shuttered in October 2001 due to a lack of trading volume.

[40] Order Revelation at Market Openings. Archishman Chakraborty, Michael Pagano, and Robert A. Schwartz. *Journal of Financial Markets*, Volume 15, Issue 2, lead article, pages 127–150, May 2012.

I have authored a couple of empirical studies on the introduction of the calls at NASDAQ, and also on the introduction of the closing call in Paris.[41] Maybe they have trouble getting order flow, but the calls significantly increase the quality of price formation. You get better prices, and you get less volatility. How do you assess the quality of prices? It's volatility, and it's tail risk. Does market quality improve? Yes, it does.

Here's one of the things I'd like to point out about the call auction. I said in my opening remarks that there is static liquidity and dynamic liquidity. When you put orders into a call auction, you harmonize the two; you can get more of both; you can get a deeper book without it impeding price discovery. In fact, a call auction facilitates price discovery. The last thing that I would like to say about this involves the supply of liquidity.

Do we have enough? How should it be supplemented? I have been arguing since the year of the 1987 crash that listed companies should be involved in the supply of liquidity for their own shares.[42] There is another source of liquidity that is just not sufficiently on the map. It is the listed companies themselves. It's sort of a startling suggestion, because General Motors, for example, is there to produce cars, not to make markets in its own stock. I am not saying that they should be making the markets but that they should be part of the liquidity supply.

Better price discovery has very broad ramifications for the economy. We call it the public good. Who is in the best position to supply this public good, to really supply that additional supplemental liquidity? We've talked about it, Greg, in relation to Bermuda. But will it ever happen? Will it happen in my lifetime? Gosh, I don't know, but, as a betting man, I wouldn't bet on it.

DOMOWITZ: Let me get you to clarify one thing.

SCHWARTZ: You've been trying for years to get me to clarify! [Laughter]

DOMOWITZ: Yes, I know, and it's a constant struggle, Bob. But when you say participate in this liquidity creation process, whether it's on the part of the companies, to me, this is also linked to the issue of whether listings actually matter in terms of liquidity. The proposal? You said you don't want them to be dealers, but you want them to somehow contribute to liquidity provision?

SCHWARTZ: I will try to summarize it as quickly as I can, but obviously, there are multiple facets. Basically, a company would establish a fund to be run by a broker/dealer, not by the company. The fund would operate by injecting orders into the market whenever the market is called. The buy/sell orders should be entered into the call auctions only. It would help seed the calls. It would improve the operations of

---

[41] A Call Auction's Impact on Price Formation and Order Routing: Evidence from the Nasdaq Stock Market. Michael S. Pagano, Lin Peng, and Robert A. Schwartz. *Journal of Financial Markets*, May, 2013.

A Closing Call's Impact on Market Quality at Euronext Paris. Michael S. Pagano and Robert A. Schwartz, *Journal of Financial Economics*, 68, 2003, pp. 439–484.

[42] A Proposal to Stabilize Stock Prices. Robert A. Schwartz. *Journal of Portfolio Management,* Fall 1988, pp. 4–11. Translated into Italian and published in *Rivista Della Borsa,* August 1989. Reprinted in *Journal of Trading*, Volume 4, Number 2, Spring 2009, pp. 50–57.

the calls. It will increase the stabilization efficiencies of the orders. The company would be buying in a falling market and selling in a rising market.

Empirically, we find that, with the excess volatility that occurs in the markets, prices bounce around and mean reversion dominates trending. Consequently, we find that the stabilization funds, for the most part, actually generate profits for the stabilization funds.[43]

DOMOWITZ: It's interesting. Because as a member of the executive committee of a public company, ITG, I certainly can say without reservation that if I simply set up something where we arbitrarily traded our own stock, we'd actually have a bit of a problem, from a legal and regulatory point of view.[44]

EDWARDS: I can explain briefly how the programs that exist currently work.

It's a little more direct in Europe than it is in the US. In the US, you would pay a higher listing fee, and the exchange would manage paying out to the market maker if the market maker meets certain qualifications. If they are not providing additional liquidity, they don't get any of that money. The money doesn't go back to the issuer, but they're paying an additional fee in listing fees to the exchange. In Europe, it's slightly more direct, but the exchange is still the intermediary.

DOMOWITZ: You know that if it's market making, it's not the exchange. Let's differentiate there. We're well beyond the days when the two were synonymous.[45]

SCHWARTZ: But it is the designated market makers in Europe, and, Robert [Barnes], you know all about that.

BARNES: Yes.

DOMOWITZ: Then the question that arises is a more general one with respect to liquidity provision. I mean, do you still believe in incentives? The question really is, do you need to incent a broker by offering the broker trading privileges others do not enjoy in order to get them to post prices? In other words, the fact that someone needs to incent means that fundamentally, the pricing mechanism for supplying liquidity is market failure because otherwise, you would not incent.

In your business, do you think about it as incentives to people to get stuff on the book?

DOVE: There are incentives to participating in the marketplace. In our market, we expect to attract a wide range of trading strategies and investor types. Many of those will be people who are looking for price discontinuities or inefficiencies.[46]

---

[43] A Proposal to Stabilize Stock Prices. Robert A. Schwartz *Journal of Portfolio Management.* Fall 1988, pp. 4–11.

[44] In a sidenote after the conference, Ian Domowitz noted to how a public company must trade its stock on a public venue like an exchange or an ATS, and the trading must be done through a broker.

The acquisition of ITG by Virtu Financial was completed on March 1, 2019. https://www.virtu.com/

[45] As Ian Domowitz noted in a follow-up, exchanges do not "make markets," by putting out bids and offers; only broker-dealers do that, and some have privileges in return for obligations to set prices through the bid and offer process.

[46] The speaker is referring to how the market reacts to liquidity and in particular the reaction of market participants, with prices rising and falling and moving about in response to the availability of liquidity.

They will be looking to capitalize on those, and I think especially so in a new marketplace like ours. In many ways, it's more attractive for those types of trading strategies to be implemented in a new marketplace like ours because there are more of these discontinuities.

DOMOWITZ: I certainly am a believer there. I was trying to get at the idea that you would give money or privileges to a market maker if, indeed, that person was willing to make markets in the stock.

DOVE: We don't have market makers in our model. We do have sort of lead traders who would specialize in certain classes of risk. They may have different types of information and may be able to have access to initial offerings of new contracts when they do come into the marketplace.

DOMOWITZ: What do you think, Robert?

BARNES: In Europe and other parts of the globe, we actually have negative interest rates. Increasingly, in this interest rate environment today, there is the search by investors for yield and buying and selling opportunities. In this regard, let me share a few statistics on Turquoise.

In just the last 3 years, value traded, denominated in euros, on our lit order book, Turquoise Lit Order Book, has more than doubled. On our dark pool, Turquoise Plato, value traded, denominated in euros, has actually more than tripled.[47]

What's even more eye-opening is the number of stock symbols that are actually trading. Three years ago, 2013, there were 1600 different stock names that were routinely trading on the Turquoise platform. Today, there are 2600 different stock names. Why does that matter? Because, ladies and gentlemen, when we consider that, in Europe, 80 percent of all the value that trades on all the order books every day is in just the top 300 blue chips. It means investors are looking for choice in order to get their business done.[48]

Our efforts at Turquoise to extend the geographic scope of investments to include the emerging markets is also interesting. Turquoise is unique amongst the European platforms and the alternate venues. In our stock universe, we have added the stocks of emerging countries to include the Czech Republic, Hungary, and Poland. This month, we have just launched the midpoint matching engine called Turquoise Plato, for the Czech Republic and Hungary.

Why does that matter? Because when we look to, say, the developed UK, bid offer spreads are about two to five basis points wide. But in the blue chips of the Czech Republic and Hungary, they can be anywhere from 10 to 30 basis points plus.

[47] https://www.platopartnership.com/about-turquoise-plato

[48] As of writing, Turquoise has more than 4000 stock symbols available for trading. Not every stock is active. According to Robert Barnes, across all stock exchanges in Europe and alternate regulated venues like Turquoise, the daily value traded in Euros is concentrated as he notes in his remarks, approximately 80 percent, in the top 300 blue chips across all markets.

Robert Barnes added in a follow-up: "After the equivalent of Quantitative Easing in Europe, which led to negative interest rates, we started to observe that the number of stock symbols that became active each month grew from approximately 1600 in 2013 to something in excess of 3000 today, as investors seeking growth widened the number of stocks to include more and more mid- and small-caps."

Of course, if we go down even into the developed small-caps, it's not uncommon to get into hundred basis points plus in bid offer spreads. Here is what is positive about all of this at Turquoise: Being able on our platform to offer execution channels that meet regulatory requirements, that allows the investor to do business but at a lower cost, and to allow the investor to do business but maybe even generate some more revenue.

To answer your specific question about paying an incentive up front to a market maker, modulating that through a tariff structure or through a structural model, it really comes down to an appropriate structural model as demonstrated by Turquoise.

DOMOWITZ: It depends on who pays. Now this is very embarrassing for a moderator. I don't have a watch, and I turned off my phone. Can someone call time, please, for me!

SCHWARTZ: You have another 3 minutes!

DOMOWITZ: Three minutes?

SCHWARTZ: If you ask the right question. [Laughter]

DOMOWITZ: If I ask the right question, all right. I need to ask a question just because it's of current interest, not necessarily because it's the expertise of this panel. But we have a lot of smart people here.

There is a lot of talk about multi-asset exchange structures, especially as we've seen OTC markets migrate to something that is much more exchange-like. I think foreign exchange, FX, is a great example. You even have ATSs that are offering equities in any currency that you want, and they're handling the FX part of that trade for you, should it be desired.

From a liquidity point of view, do you see value in so-called multi-asset exchange structures under the assumption that you can trade the instrument on an exchange? I don't mean necessarily registered here. I'm thinking anything that centralizes as opposed to the pure OTC model?

SCHWARTZ: I see two things in the question. As Will and Greg are doing, the socioeconomic value of bringing liquidity to an instrument is tremendous. And this is part of what I was thinking of when I structured the panel. When acquiring liquidity, how you get it is terribly important.

Here's the other aspect of your question. I wonder if implicitly you're asking if there's an interaction effect which makes the whole greater than the sum of the parts?

DOMOWITZ: From a liquidity point of view, yes.

SCHWARTZ: Yes, and I don't know the answer to the second one. But to the first, it's very big.

DOMOWITZ: Greg, do you want to take a whack at that?

WOJCIECHOWSKI: It depends on your business model as an exchange. In our experience, the BSX's business model is doing something different. We see the limitations of our small market. How do we design a regulated marketplace that does all the things that a more traditional marketplace does, one that's been operating for decades, and bringing that to a new asset class that needs liquidity? That's what Will is looking at. That's what we're looking at. And there needs to be, additionally, from our perspective, a niche market for insurance-related securities.

How do you get the capital markets more comfortable with deploying their capital into a risk structured product? Our response to that is that you create the infrastructure around it, that the market be aware of it, and that they feel comfortable with it. In our case, cat bonds—catastrophe bonds—are something that we're seeing an awful lot of uptick on or uptake on our exchange.

That would be developing liquidity in an otherwise really opaque asset class that has a huge amount of potential to grow. That's a great question because I think there will be exchanges like our exchange in Bermuda that will focus on niche products, or niche asset classes, that need the capital market support that may not, you know, enjoy it. The level of discussion here today is a reflection of just how to unlock that new liquidity that might potentially be out there.

The answer to the question of new liquidity is about liquidity that might be part of a pool that will end up as a new asset class. That in turn will generate new investment opportunities.

DOMOWITZ: I'm going to leave the last one to Amy, especially since even that suggestion starts to cross regulatory lines, in the US. That would be the CFTC and the SEC I think.

EDWARDS: As an economist, I like to say that there are lots of different kinds of markets. But fundamentally, at their core, they are markets.

SCHWARTZ: Markets are markets.

EDWARDS: Yes, markets are markets. That said, there are differences in the dynamics between different types of instruments. If we go full circle back to where you started at the beginning, Ian, there's a history. The history shows that a lot of financial assets did trade on the same exchanges. Look at how the New York Stock Exchange started. You know, 100 years ago, they traded fixed income and trading migrated according to the dynamics and where people wanted to trade those instruments. We still have some exchanges that trade both options and equities.

There are some places where you get different financial assets that trade in the same places. But you have this migration that seems to be natural within the market.

DOMOWITZ: Since I was told 3 minutes, we've run ourselves out. I want to thank the panel. We can follow up with them later over cocktails.

Chapter 6
Fireside Chat: Michael S. Piwowar, Commissioner, Securities and Exchange Commission

Robert A. Schwartz, Larry Tabb, and Michael S. Piwowar

LARRY TABB: The conference today is about liquidity. My first question for Michael Piwowar is how do you look at the SEC's role in the creation of liquidity? Are you mostly, in fact, really looking at trying to regulate the transfer of liquidity?

MICHAEL PIWOWAR: Thank you Larry. First, let me say, it's rare for me to actually stay for an entire conference as I have done today. I have been here since the start of this conference. I have learned something new from every single panel, which is a reflection of some very fine debate.

I brought one of my counsels with me. She's here to remind me I have to do my disclaimer, just like Amy Edwards did earlier at this conference.[1] Any ideas I express are my own and do not necessarily reflect the views of the Commission, nor my fellow commissioners. If you see my votes, they often do not reflect the views of my fellow commissioners.

On your question, Larry, about liquidity, my answer is yes. On a daily basis, there are issues that come up for us at the Commission that relate to liquidity. Enough has been said about the tick-size pilot and about the equity space.[2] On the

---

[1] See Chap. 5: New Approaches to Creating Liquidity. The panelists included Amy Edwards of the US Securities and Exchange Commission.

[2] See Investor Alert. Tick Size Pilot Program. What Investors Need to Know. Securities and Exchange Commission. October 03, 2016. https://www.sec.gov/oiea/investor-alerts-bulletins/ia_ticksize.html

---

R. A. Schwartz (✉)
Zicklin School of Business, Baruch College - CUNY, New York, NY, USA
e-mail: robert.schwartz@baruch.cuny.edu

L. Tabb
Tabb Group, New York, NY, USA

M. S. Piwowar
U.S. Securities and Exchange Commission, Washington, DC, USA

R. A. Schwartz et al. (eds.), *Liquidity*, Zicklin School of Business Financial Markets Series, https://doi.org/10.1007/978-3-031-36914-8_6

last panel, Amy Edwards spoke on some of the other issues about liquidity in the equity markets that we are looking at. In the fixed-income markets, we are concerned about liquidity as well. We have primary jurisdiction over the corporate bond market and municipal bond market, and we are constantly looking at the provision of liquidity in that market.

The dynamics there are a little bit different from in the equity markets. Over time, inventory has gone down for the traditional providers of liquidity—that is, the dealers. And who are the biggest holders of bonds now, particularly corporate and municipal bonds? It's the buy-side. We've seen changes in technology. A week doesn't go by without folks reaching out to tell me about their new business model in terms of an alternative trading system in the bond markets, and of particular niches in either the corporate or municipal bond market.

And in relation to Larry's question, what are we doing at the SEC? Are we seeing our role as just monitoring liquidity or sort of promoting it? At this point, we're appropriately taking a wait-and-see approach. We have staff who are constantly looking at whether there are ways in which we can potentially enhance pre-trade transparency, particularly for retail investors in the bond market, recognizing that more transparency doesn't always necessarily mean better liquidity in these markets. We want to make sure that we get the balance right.

Then more recently, in the last couple of years, we had the Flash Crash in the treasury market.[3] That's an interesting regulatory market where the treasury has primary jurisdiction. The Federal Reserve Bank in New York and the SEC also has a role. And the three of us have been working together, along with the Commodity Futures Trading Commission, and the treasury futures market, to look at the changes in the treasury cash market.

A couple of things came out of the Flash Crash as we saw it. The regulators realized there was no real consolidated tape involved in terms of capturing all of the transactions. Recently, the SEC asked FINRA to start collecting treasury cash market transactions from broker-dealers into their trade system. To that end, we worked with the regulators to facilitate this. The Federal Reserve recently said it is going to work with FINRA to potentially require the banks to do that as well, if the trades don't occur through the broker-dealers.

The other thing we learned just piecing together some data from some different data sources is that, in fact, principal trading firms, high-frequency trading firms, are also in this market. It came as a shock to some, but not to me, knowing that these participants are out there. A lot of the same questions have been repeated for years in the equity markets concerning the role of high-frequency traders and principal trading firms. Are they dealers or not? All those same questions are now starting to come up in the government securities and in the treasury cash market. We're working with the regulators on these questions.

Then finally, an issue that may not seem like it's directly related to liquidity, but it is, relates to our investment management role, overseeing mutual funds and

[3] See Remembering the 2014 Flash Crash in Treasuries; www.etftrends.com/fixed-income-channel/remembering-the-2014-flash-crash-in-treasuries/

exchange traded funds. We've been engaged in several rulemakings, some data modernization, and those sorts of things. Recently, we went final with a liquidity risk management rule for our investment companies, the mutual funds in other words.[4]

Here is one of the concerns that folks had, particularly the prudential regulators. It is that the SEC was not regulating this market effectively, and potentially, there's threats at stake to financial stability. It makes sense for us to go out and tighten up some of our liquidity rules. In fact, we did that.

Shortly after we went out with the proposal for the rule for public comment last year, we had the Third Avenue situation. The process was interesting.[5] Folks originally thought that the Third Avenue Fund was dealing in high-yield bonds. It turns out they were involved in very, very distressed debt, very liquid securities. But for a few days, there was a concern that there will be a run on high-yield bond funds. I remember one Friday in particular, when folks on CNBC and other places were predicting this was going to be the day of the death spiral in the high-yield bond market.

Here's what did happen: Prices went down, yields went up, and then they stabilized. In the following week, we had one of our mutual funds come to us and say, Look, whatever you do in your liquidity risk rule going forward, make sure you don't create the problem you are trying to solve. So what does this mean? Their point was don't force very prescriptive rules on mutual funds in terms of maintaining the liquidity of their existing portfolio. Under discussion was the illiquid portion of the portfolio. We're now requiring firms to classify investments into highly liquid, moderate, less liquid, and illiquid. And there's a cap on the illiquid ones, so as to not force the funds to sell the illiquid funds exactly when the market starts going down.[6]

The mutual fund complex told us they were actually net buyers in the market during the Flash Crash of 2014. Their point was that they had already managed the liquidity of their portfolio very well and saw a buying opportunity. They knew they weren't going to have the outflows to sell some of their more liquid stuff and to act as the counter cyclical force in the market that day and actually buy into that market.

TABB: Basically, don't force a fire sale?

PIWOWAR: Don't force pro-cyclical regulations.[7] And that's an example of how the Commission has to make sure the left hand doesn't create liquidity problems on the right hand.

---

[4] See Investment Company Liquidity Risk Management Programs. Securities and Exchange Commission. ACTION: Final rule. October 13, 2016.
https://www.sec.gov/rules/final/2016/33-10233.pdf

[5] Third Avenue Reaches Deal with SEC Over Troubled Fund. Gregory Zuckerman. *Wall Street Journal.* December 16. 2015. https://www.wsj.com/articles/third-avenue-reaches-deal-with-sec-over-troubled-fund-1450304539

[6] See footnote 4. (ii)*Classification* beginning on Page 441 and Section (B)(4) on Page 444 of the release cited above.

[7] Broadly speaking, Piwowar is referring to the idea of regulating in response to market cycles and movements such as upturns and downturns, an approach in some markets that has been criticized for exacerbating asset prices in a manner damaging to market stability.

TABB: You talk about fixed-income markets. You're increasingly getting involved in the treasury side of that. As you said, you're working with FINRA and the Fed to kind of collect data on it. Right now, that's private. I guess that's for the regulators and the Fed. Are there views about opening that up?

PIWOWAR: To make the public transparent, yeah, absolutely. I'm an economist by training for those of you who don't know me. As far as I can tell, I am the only PhD economist to be a commissioner at the SEC. It has mostly been lawyers. And when I was at the SEC before as an economist, I worked with Amy Edwards and Larry Harris.[8] We were looking at the impacts of adding post-trade transparency to the likes of corporate bonds and municipal bonds and found it benefited retail investors in particular and that it lowered transaction costs.

On the treasury market side, there was a conference last week at the New York Fed just down the street from here at Baruch College in New York City.[9] Both SEC chair, Mary Jo White, and counsel to the treasury secretary, Antonio Weiss, teed up the issue of public dissemination in terms of prices, and the reporting of data on treasury cash market transactions. One panel talked through all the issues of whether there is potentially more institutional trading. The question raised is not whether we will have post-trade transparency in this market, but how. It's more when and how, exactly. I'm a huge proponent of that. And I am also a huge proponent of historical data products for academicians to conduct research studies.

At this same conference at the New York Fed, one panel raised the issue of off-the-run securities and the role of the fed.[10]

---

[8] SEC Names Larry Harris New Chief Economist. Douglass Gore. *USC News.* https://news.usc.edu/3001/SEC-Names-Larry-Harris-New-Chief-Economist/

[9] See Conference on Treasury Market Structure, October 24, 2016. The Evolving Structure of the US Treasury Market: Second Annual Conference.

"The conference, jointly organized by the U.S. Department of the Treasury, the Federal Reserve Board, the Federal Reserve Bank of New York, the U.S. Securities and Exchange Commission (SEC), and the U.S. Commodity Futures Trading Commission (CFTC), was attended by domestic and international representatives from the official sector, the press, academia, and the private sector. Key issues discussed included (i) official comments on progress regarding Treasury market reform and priorities, (ii) the reporting of data on Treasury cash market transactions, (iii) Treasury secondary market clearing practices, (iv) the future of Treasury market settlement, and (v) the evolution of Treasury market structure."

https://www.newyorkfed.org/medialibrary/media/newsevents/events/markets/2016/treasury-market-conference-summary-2016.pdf?la=en

Source: New York Fed.

[10] Off-the-run treasuries refer to any treasury security that has been issued, except for the newest issue, which are called on-the-run. Off-the-run treasuries tend to be somewhat less liquid than on-the-run securities, although they are still actively traded on the secondary market. Source: Investopedia.

"Several panelists voiced the expectation that in five years, there could be very liquid, all-to-all electronic trading of on-the-run securities. By contrast, with respect to off-the-run securities, one panelist said that a functioning Treasury market may require either the Treasury or the Fed to provide some kind of 'liquidity solution' for these securities (for example, via daily auctions). Several panelists noted that they expect the innovations that have changed the on-the-run securities market over the past few years to start to emerge in the off-the-run sector. Panelists emphasized the 'spe-

TABB: Robert Barnes, on the last panel, mentioned how the number of corporate issues—and I'm assuming they're not just ETFs but the corporate issues—has expanded fairly significantly over the last 5 years.[11] How do you see us trying to get back to an era where we're adding more corporate issues to the tape?

PIWOWAR: For a long time, we noticed that companies are staying private longer. The question is why? A couple of years ago, Congress tried to address some of the concerns through the JOBS Act.[12] One piece is called the IPO On-Ramp, which instead of having the cliff effect when you go public, all of a sudden your regulatory burden is going straight up instead.[13] Emerging growth companies have a period of up to 5 years in terms of regulatory burden.[14] It applies to companies with up to a total of 1 billion dollars in annual revenue, and there's a scaled approach to regulation in this case. If, in fact, the costs of going public were so high and that the cliff effect was too high, maybe some firms would, with the new regulation, start going public that way. That is the idea here.

The other thing the IPO On-Ramp did was de-risk some of the going public process.[15] Some of the concerns that biotech companies in particular had was that when companies go public and put their first S1 in their first prospectus with the SEC, it goes on EDGAR and becomes live right away.[16] And everybody gets to see it, including the rivals, right? And it's proprietary information; it's out there. It's a back

---

cial' status of the Treasury market as compared with other asset classes' markets (for example, the equity market)."

Source:https://www.newyorkfed.org/medialibrary/media/newsevents/events/markets/2016/treasury-market-conference-summary-2016.pdf?la=en

Source: New York Fed.

[11] See Chap. 5, New Approaches for Creating Liquidity.

[12] Jumpstart Our Business Startups (JOBS) Act https://www.sec.gov/spotlight/jobs-act.shtml

[13] JOBS Act Provides IPO "On-Ramp" for Emerging Growth Companies. The new JOBS Act (Jumpstart Our Business Startups Act), a package of bills aimed at providing easier access to capital for new and emerging companies, was signed into law by President Obama. Although the "crowd-funding" provisions of the JOBS Act have been widely reported, one of the more helpful capital-raising provisions of the JOBS Act may prove to be the so-called "on-ramp" provisions designed to allow easier access to the IPO market for emerging growth companies (EGCs), private companies with total annual gross revenues of less than $1 billion in their last fiscal year. Title I of the JOBS Act, which is effective now, reduces the disclosure, reporting, and regulatory burdens under federal securities that would otherwise apply to an EGC in the registration process and for a transition period of up to 5 years thereafter.

Source: Current Developments in Securities Laws. Blank Rome LLP. April 2012. www.blankrome.com/siteFiles/UptoDate-4-apr12.pdf

See IPO On-Ramp Provisions. *Ward & Smith.* September 19. 2014. https://www.wardandsmith.com/articles/ipo-on-ramp-provisions

[14] Ibid.

[15] The Secret Behind "De-Risking" IPOs). Alyx Flournoy. *Omega Point Blog*. September 27, 2020. https://blog.ompnt.com/the-secret-behind-de-risking-ipos

[16] A Form S1, commonly referred to as the "Prospectus" or simply the "S1," is the official Securities and Exchange Commission ("SEC") document your company must file to register its securities with the SEC. Registering securities with the SEC enables a company to offer its securities to the public in an IPO. Source: ipohub.org

and forth with the Division for Corporation Finance at the SEC to make sure that they address certain issues and that all of those become public in the going public process.

We heard of a lot of firms that didn't want to give up that information right away to their rivals since it would give them a head start and because it would take sometimes weeks and months to go public. The IPO On-Ramp allowed firms to do confidential filings. The original filing and the amendments stayed private until a certain number of days before going public. The idea is to allow enough time for investors to see it, but not so much time that your rivals can front run you. And that has been extremely successful. We saw something like 80 biotech companies go public immediately after this.

This suggests that Congress got it right on the de-risking piece of the IPO On-Ramp, that we got it right in that piece, and so did the folks who put it together. But outside of that industry, we're still not seeing a lot of folks going public. That suggests there is still other regulatory impediments to going public. Is it just simply because the liquidity is not there? That's why we're talking about the tick-size pilot. And other folks have suggested that there is not a lot of research or marketing that's going on out there.

Industry participants were highly critical of the tick-size pilot in some of the earlier sessions. They're all fair criticisms. I, myself, have been skeptical of what some of the proponents think will be the ultimate outcome of the tick-size pilot.

My standard joke is that then the sell-side analysts from 1994 reappear.[17] I mean it's kind of that view of the world. What we've learned from this conference, and at other places, is that the providers of liquidity today are different than the providers in the past. And so it's a different sort of thing, in that sense.

Now having said that, I still think it's a good idea for us to do the pilot for a number of reasons. For one, Congress was going to tell us to do it. There was a bill working its way through Congress that would have mandated us to do it. It was highly prescriptive; it was a 5-year plan, which would have allowed firms to opt in. And for those of you who are academic researchers, you just cringe at that. You have here a huge endogeneity, self-selection problem, and all kinds of other research design problems.[18]

TABB: There were discussions about companies being able to control their own tick size and stuff like that.

PIWOWAR: All kinds of stuff. We wanted to have a simple pilot program that we could control. On the one hand, we've heard we're starting to get results right away, and we knew that was going to happen. That suggests you do a shorter pilot

[17] As one attendee wryly noted after listening to the speaker: "The horse is out of the barn! 1994 was the heyday of the sell-side research analyst." He added: "Since then their ranks have dwindled and nothing we do will bring them back."

[18] In a statistical model, a parameter or variable is said to be endogenous when there is a correlation between the parameter or variable and the error term. Endogeneity can arise as a result of measurement error, autoregression with autocorrelated errors, simultaneity, and omitted variables. Source: definitions.net

program. On the other hand, we were hearing folks say, Well, these were low liquidity stocks at stake anyway. I'm just going to sit this one out. You have to be careful when you design a pilot program in the sense that you end up getting the results that you would want from this stuff. We designed it for a two-year time span, knowing that we will fully get results in the meantime. After one year, I'd like to hold a roundtable, gather up everybody with research on it, the academics and industry professionals. We can look at the results so that we then have a 1-year lead time before this thing ends to decide whether to just let it finally end, make it permanent, or do something different.

TABB: The way it stands, there is now a two-year kind of window, but there is nothing to say that in two-years plus a day, this whole thing reverts back to normal, right?

PIWOWAR: Right.

TABB: It must be like the penny pilot on options that go on forever?[19]

PIWOWAR: I know there's some pilot programs at the SEC that are older than my kids. My former colleague, Dan Gallagher, used to call them *Frankenpilots*. These things just go on forever. That's why I want to make sure that one year in, we get a good idea of what we will do at the end of this latest pilot. Maybe we decide to make it permanent. I'd like to have the conversation about letting firms choose their tick size. Maybe we decide that firms are bucketed based on their average daily volume over the past six months, that they get put into buckets for tick size. There was discussion earlier in today's conference about the high liquidity stocks. Maybe there's a case for lowering the tick size for those.

TABB: Be a little bit more flexible.

PIWOWAR: Exactly. The worst thing that would happen is we just keep going on and on and on, and it becomes one of those *Frankenpilots*. The other thing would be to turn it off, wait six months, and then decide that it is a good idea and turn it back on again. Then folks have to reprogram and reprogram, and all that sort of costly stuff.

TABB: You've had a pretty aggressive agenda the last couple of years. Now you have the Equity Market Structure Committee.[20] What's your take on that process? It was a little skeptical, but it seems like they've done some good work.

---

[19] "Prior to 2007, most options traded with minimum price variations (MPVs) of $.05 for premiums below $3.00 and $.10 for premiums above $3.00. Beginning in January of 20007, the SEC initiated an industry wide (on six option exchanges) pilot program entitled the *Penny Pilot Program*, in which MPVs were reduced for certain equities. The "Pilot" reduced the MPVs to .01 for premiums below $3.00 and to .05 for premiums above $3.00. An exception to this was the ETF, QQQQ, which already traded in .01 increments.

This 6-month program which started with 13 option classes (equities) has been renewed and expanded several times": Source: The Blue Collar Investor https://www.thebluecollarinvestor.com/penny-pilot-program/

[20] See US Securities and Exchange Commission. Equity Market Structure Advisory Committee. https://www.sec.gov/spotlight/equity-market-structure-advisory-committee.shtml

PIWOWAR: Yes, they have done some very good work. They've made a lot of good recommendations. For example, there's the maker-taker access fee pilot.[21]

TABB: Will we see something there maybe?

PIWOWAR: Possibly, I hope so. Actually. There are a few questions. If we decide to do something, can we start that pilot before the end of the tick-size pilot? Even though they will be fundamentally different securities, are there any odd spill-over effects that we will see from there?

The other thing to consider is programmatic. How do we do the pilot? The tick-size pilot was done under what's called an NMS plan. At the SEC, that means we put out an order telling the SROs and the exchanges to go out and design a plan and then come back.[22] And we kind of say yes, no, and go back and forth. The other way, we just do a rule that specifies it at the SEC. We put it out for public comment. In response to the public comment, we then go forward with the final rulemaking.

The benefit of doing the NMS plan is this: You get started earlier because we basically just say go forth and figure this stuff out, in contrast to a rulemaking basis where we have to do a lot of upfront, thoughtful processes in terms of cost benefit analysis, going through all the alternatives, and that sort of stuff.

Having said that, if we do the rulemaking process, we get to an end a lot quicker because with an NMS plan, I spend a lot of meetings with folks from the SROs and others who aren't part of the conversation and say, Hey, we think it should have this; we think it should have that, it should not have this; and it should not have that. I'd rather make it part of a full public comment process.

TABB: One of the big things we saw last year was that IEX became an exchange.[23] And now there's a whole bunch of other folks with different plans. What's your thought on speed bumps?[24] Where are we going to go? And how has this worked out so far?

PIWOWAR: It was interesting. If you looked at the public comment file, the IEX exchange application basically, at some point, became sort of a referendum on Reg NMS which is a great thing. Because Tim Mahoney in an earlier panel today mentioned how my predecessor at the SEC, Dan Gallagher, had called for a holistic

---

[21] See update June 17, 2020: Appeals Court Tosses SEC's Maker-Taker Pilot. Thomson Reuters Tax & Accounting.

https://tax.thomsonreuters.com/news/appeals-court-tosses-secs-maker-taker-pilot/

[22] The NMS plan is what participants, such as an exchange, agree to participate in for a variety of matters. For instance, there are NMS plans for market data, symbology, the consolidated audit trail (CAT), circuit breakers, and more. See FINRA. https://www.finra.org/rules-guidance/guidance/national-market-system-plans

[23] IEX Begins Operation as an Exchange Following Interpretive Guidance Adopted by the SEC. *Sidley Publications*. September 6, 2016 https://www.sidley.com/en/insights/newsupdates/2016/09/iex-begins-operation

[24] Opinion: Speed Bumps Are the Hot New Thing for Exchanges.

Stock markets are customizing delays for executing trades. That's going to make things pretty messy. *Bloomberg*. Matt Levine. August 31, 2016

https://www.bloomberg.com/opinion/articles/2016-08-31/speed-bumps-are-the-hot-new-thing-for-exchanges

review of market structure.[25] I've done the same thing. I've actually put forth a plan in terms of how we should do it, modeled after the 1963 study that Ian Domowitz discussed on the last panel today, the Special Study of Securities Markets.[26] It was in the middle of that study when the 1962 Flash Crash happened, and they just added another chapter onto it as a result, which is kind of cool. And then at the same time, we also saw a program in the UK where the government worked with academics and market participants to leverage a lot of the work that's out there. It turns out that if you give academics enough data, they'll do a heck of a lot of work for free. This is a good thing because they get other benefits out of that as well.

In fact, I've been calling again, for a review of Reg NMS. We have something called the Regulatory Flexibility Act, an Act that requires us to review rules and their effects on small entities.[27] Every year, we have to put together a list of rules that we're going to evaluate under the Reg Flexibility Act. When we put it out for public comment, on average, we get zero comments. But this year in September, we put out our list and it included Reg NMS. So I put out a statement, which was picked up by some newspapers. I said, Look, here's a referendum on Reg NMS, here's an opportunity for everybody, including industry participants and others inside and outside this room, that says we need to do a more comprehensive review of market structure. Here's the vehicle in which we can do it. The Regulatory Flexibility Act forces us to go back and look at this stuff. We're asking for public comment on this. If you start giving us public comment on these, the big picture items we want you to look at, we can't ignore that. It's going to force us to be responsive to the public comments, which is exactly what you want from your regulators. If you have those ideas, add them into the public comment. And if you don't, then a pox on all your houses!

TABB: If we got enough votes, could we really repeal Reg NMS?

PIWOWAR: I mean I don't know about repeal, but at least we could do a comprehensive study on market structure. Back to your question about IEX. On that one, it's a matter of public record. On the exchange application for IEX, I joined with my colleagues and voted in favor of approving IEX as an exchange. But I dissented on the piece that allowed them to have protected quote status under Reg NMS.[28] If we want to have a conversation about this, we want to consider maybe a *de minimis* exemption—an exception to a program delay or an intentional delay

[25] See Chap. 2. How Technology Is Transforming Liquidity Provision.

[26] See Chap. 5. New Approaches for Creating Liquidity.

[27] The Regulatory Flexibility Act (RFA) of 1980 is a law designed to make government agencies review all regulations that they impose to ensure that they do not place a disproportionate economic burden on small business owners and other small entities.
Source: Regulatory Flexibility Act | Inc.com.

[28] See Protected Quote & Waive-in Membership Deadline | IEX
iextrading.com/trading/alerts/2016/052/

which is in the rule.[29] If you think back to the protected quote status and the fast and slow markets debate, it was really about the New York Stock Exchange floor. Now the technology has changed. One could argue, and I agree, that it didn't contemplate any of these sort of geographic latencies and the nanoseconds and microsecond speed of trading.[30]

But rather than deal with it on a case-by-case basis, we need to have a policy decision on the speed bumps in general.[31] We need to have the benefit of public comment on that. That is my view.

TABB: You recently sent out a proposal to extend Rule 605/606 in regard to greater transparency. How is that going? Will we see more institutional transparency in the marketplace?[32]

PIWOWAR: I hope we see more transparency. On the institutional side, we don't really have any right now. We put a proposal out for public comment.[33]

Jim Angel was here earlier.[34] He wrote a thoughtful comment telling us we got it completely wrong and should have put a lot of other things in there. Bob Schwartz mentioned this. I am a former academic as well. We need more public comment from academics in this space.

We're getting comments from a lot of industry folks, the market participants. We need the academics to tell us, If you have data items, or if you had this particular frequency of data, what type of research could you do that would then shine a light on things. For example, is the provision of liquidity and execution quality driving folks' decisions of where they route their orders? Answer these sorts of fundamental questions: What can we do to improve transparency?

I hope we quickly move forward with our proposal.

---

[29] See Market Integrity Insights 24 Mar 2016.

IEX Exchange Application: SEC's Reassessment of Reg NMS Critical to Decision. Rhodri G. Preece, Market Integrity Insights. CFA. March 24, 2016.

www.cfainstitute.org/en/advocacy/market-integrity-insights/2016/03/iex-exchange-application-secs-reassessment-of-reg-nms-critical-to-decision

[30] This refers to the ability of market participants to gain advantages in the speed of their trade executions and price-quote data through advanced technology, specifically the "colocation" of their computer servers near stock exchanges' computers. That lowers so-called latency, a critical factor in high-speed trade executions. The practice is regarded as legal though it has many critics. This helps explain Piwowar's reference to the New York Stock Exchange.

See Understanding High-Frequency Trading Terminology investopedia.com/articles/active-trading/042414/youd-better-know-your-highfrequency-trading-terminology.asp

[31] More Exchanges Add "Speed Bumps," Defying High-Frequency Traders. Axexander Osipovich. *Wall Street Journal*. July 29, 2019 https://www.wsj.com/articles/more-exchanges-add-speed-bumps-defying-high-frequency-traders-11564401611

[32] SEC.gov | Division of Trading and Markets Disclosure of Order Execution and Order Routing Information (Rules 605 and 606 of Regulation NMS) [formerly Rules 11Ac1-5 and 11Ac1-6] www.sec.gov/divisions/marketreg/disclosure.htm

[33] See footnote 32.

[34] Professor Jim Angel, Georgetown University, specializes in the market structure and regulation of global financial markets.

TABB: Are you going to follow Europe in terms of trying to get folks to unbundle?[35] I guess the maker-taker tries to look at incentives and their impact on routing.[36] How aggressive do you think the SEC will be along those lines?

PIWOWAR: I hope not. I hope we don't go down that path. From my view, I like pilot programs; I like experiments. I think Europe will give us a natural experiment in this area. We can learn from what goes well and what doesn't go so well from this sort of thing.

TABB: We saw the Department of Labor come out with a Fiduciary Rule trying to move ERISA accounts away from a suitability standard on brokerage accounts to more of a situation where the broker or advisor needs to be a fiduciary.[37] Your thoughts on that first? Second, is there a discussion, and what are your thoughts on trying to do that for the taxable world rather than the ERISA world?

PIWOWAR: For folks who maybe aren't as familiar as others, this is the DOL fiduciary rule under ERISA.[38] We don't administer ERISA; this is where the DOL administers. We have a highly fragmented regulatory framework. Unfortunately, Dodd-Frank not only didn't make it better; it actually made it worse.[39] It added to the alphabet soup of regulators.

And one of the issues we're constantly dealing with is overlapping jurisdictions. And the DOL did this rule that not only affects ERISA, but it also affects our brokers who are talking to their customers about IRA accounts and those types of things.[40]

TABB: As well as fund managers, too?

PIWOWAR: Fund managers and all that sort of stuff. In terms of the DOL Fiduciary Duty Rule, I think it's terrible, horrible, no good, a very bad rule.

---

[35] FLASH FRIDAY: From Unbundling to Rebundling—Traders Magazine—Tourmaline Partners. https://www.tourmalinellc.com/press/2020/9/28/flash-friday-from-unbundling-to-rebundling-traders-magazine

Source: Tourmaline Partners September 28, 2020.

[36] In a competitive program to encourage trading on exchanges, maker-taker fees offer a transaction rebate to trading participants who provide liquidity, charging customers who take liquidity.

Read more: What Maker-Taker Fees Mean To You | Source: Investopedia.com http://www.investopedia.com/articles/active-trading/042414/what-makertaker-fees-mean-you.asp#ixzz4IvzckkIR

[37] Everything You Need to Know About the DOL Fiduciary Rule. https://www.investopedia.com/updates/dol-fiduciary-rule/updates/dol-fiduciary-rule/

Source: Katelyn Peters. Investopedia.

Updated July 14, 2021.

DOL Updates the Fiduciary Rule (Again). Jana Steele. Callan. October 18. 2021.

www.callan.com/blog-archive/fiduciary-rule-updates/

[38] Ibid.

[39] The Dodd-Frank Wall Street Reform and Consumer Protection Act is a massive piece of financial reform legislation passed during the Obama administration in 2010 as a response to the financial crisis of 2008. Named after sponsors Sen. Christopher J. Dodd (D-Conn.) and Rep. Barney Frank (D-Mass.), the act contains numerous provisions, spelled out over roughly 2300 pages, that were to be implemented over a period of several years.

[40] DOL Fiduciary Rule: What Employers Should Know | NPPG-FS www.nppg.com/news/fiduciary-rule/

TABB: But don't be honest.

PIWOWAR: I know, that's right. It is a horrible rule. There are folks that have teams of lawyers looking at this rule trying to figure out how to comply, and just when they think they figure it out in one section of the rule, then they look at another section of the rule. And they find out they can't comply. For a while folks thought, the robo-advisor-style approach would be sort of the way to go. That doesn't look like it's going to work.

Those of us who like good public policy think it's a terrible, horrible, no good, very bad rule. But for the folks who intended it to be that type of rule, it's fantastic. It was intended for one thing, and that was to help trial lawyers, period. It was not intended to help investors in any way, whatsoever. If you look at it from that perspective, it's a fantastic rule for some but not for others. These aren't unintended consequences; these are intended consequences.

TABB: Basically, the trial lawyers want somebody with deep pockets that they can sue.

PIWOWAR: Exactly. Look at what's happening in the industry right now. Merrill Lynch came out a couple of weeks ago saying they can't do commission-based stuff. Morgan Stanley said maybe we think we can, but we're not sure how we want to do it.[41] We see other folks, retail brokers, thinking about doing robo-advisors.[42] But then the Secretary of State in Massachusetts says we're not so sure that digital or robo-advisor-type meets our duty, our fiduciary standard in this state. And we have other types of things. It's a mess.

TABB: As long as you sit on the Commission, are you voting against any type of DOL standard for taxable accounts?[43]

PIWOWAR: Absolutely right. Even before the DOL came in, the SEC has been wrestling this for a long time. You have the brokers who have had their traditional business model and commission-based business. There is the investment advisors with the traditional business model and asset and other management-based compensation. Over the years, the business lines have blurred so people have been calling for us to figure this out because there are two different statutes. If you're a broker,

---

[41] See update Merrill Lynch reviewing ban on commissions-paying retirement accounts. Reuters. June 15, 2015.

https://www.investing.com/news/stock-market-news/merrill-lynch-reviewing-ban-on-commissionspaying-retirement-accounts-1495323

See update DOL Fiduciary Rule a "Positive" for Morgan Stanley, Says Wealth Boss. Mason Braswell *AdvisorHub*. May 31, 2017.

https://www.advisorhub.com/dol-fiduciary-rule-positive-morgan-stanley-says-wealth-boss/

[42] Robo-advisors (also spelled robo-adviser or roboadvisor) are digital platforms that provide automated, algorithm-driven financial planning services with little to no human supervision. A typical robo-advisor collects information from clients about their financial situation and future goals through an online survey and then uses the data to offer advice and automatically invest client assets. Source: Investopedia.

[43] Taxable Brokerage Accounts vs IRA: What's Better? | SoFi.

www.sofi.com/learn/content/what-is-a-taxable-account/

you come under the '34 Act and the FINRA rule book.[44] If you're an investment advisor, you have a fiduciary standard and not the FINRA rule. Nevertheless, there's case law on both sides. Is there a way for us to harmonize that?

A few years ago, the RAND IABD study commissioned by the SEC had some interesting findings.[45] For one, investors were confused about the standard of industry care. When professionals call themselves advisors, that does not tell us about the standard of care. These same professionals have to ask themselves the question, Are they an investment advisor or a registered broker-dealer?

For another matter, investors were generally happy with the care that they got even though they were confused. So for me, before we moved to rulemaking that potentially upsets decades of rules and court cases, and all these other sorts of matters, we need to do a couple of things.

First, we need to make sure if the confusion leads to worse outcomes. Is it the case that people who are more confused, maybe less sophisticated, get worse outcomes? Do they get worse advice than other investors? Are their risk-adjusted returns worse than others? And even if that's the case, before we move to rulemaking, can we engage in education, point-of-sale disclosure, or something like that to get at this issue? It's a really hard question we've been wrestling with.

TABB: From an outside perspective, it just makes me think that it will push me away from getting less expensive advice. The people who need advice who don't have a whole lot of assets under management just basically get cut off. In this regard, in talking to brokers, it seems like they're just going to cut off a whole bunch of people.

PIWOWAR: That's exactly it. We've seen this at the forefront in the UK in the RDR review.[46] At stake is this: Once you raise the cost of compliance per account, then the break-even point in terms of assets and account balances goes way up. And there is something like 9 or 10 million households in the UK that are now priced out of the market. And this was the concern of the DOL fiduciary rule early on. You had members of Congress from rural communities worried about the provision of advice. You also had the Congressional Black Caucus worried about it in minority urban communities as well, too.

TABB: And they just ignored them all.

PIWOWAR: And they just ignored them all. They would just roll over them on that. I mean if you just keep raising the cost of compliance, folks start exiting the business. You are not going to get any of that stuff. And the thing that worries me most of all as a regulator is that six years after Dodd-Frank, folks don't realize we're

---

[44] Securities Exchange Act of 1934.
Will Kenton. Updated October 30, 2020.
www.investopedia.com/terms/s/seact1934.asp

[45] See SEC's RAND Study Released. Christina Mucciolo. Wealthmanagement.com. Jan 03, 2008.
www.wealthmanagement.com/opinions/sec-s-rand-study-released

[46] Understanding the retail distribution review (RDR) | Find A Wealth Manager.
findawealthmanager.com/knowledge/retail-distribution-review-rdr/

not done with all the rulemaking yet.[47] We're only about two-thirds of the way done. Think about that. And of that two-thirds, the compliance costs haven't even really started to bite yet. It's not any single rule; it's the accumulation of rules.

TABB: We're starting to see some folks say, Hey, look, maybe we've gone too far. Are you starting to hear that in Washington?

PIWOWAR: People say it quietly to me. Nobody wants to admit this publicly. But no, I meet with folks all the time. This idea that it's the cumulative effect, and you can't pin it to any one thing in particular. I was talking to somebody earlier about, hey, can you comment on what I said about Reg NMS? They said I've got eight other things to comment on right now! It's just the onslaught of rules that are coming down the pipeline, particularly from Dodd-Frank. Folks are just kind of catch as you can, and you can't really stop all this stuff. And we haven't seen the cumulative effect.

There's an economist, Michael Mandel, who used this beautiful analogy of pebbles in a stream. If you think of the economy flowing like a stream, you throw one pebble into it, no big deal, but if you throw enough pebbles, you finally stop the flow of the stream. And you say, Well, whoa, what stopped the water from flowing? You can't pinpoint it to any one thing. It was just the onslaught of all those things. And we, as regulators, are mandated to look at the costs and benefits of any rule. But we do it in isolation. So we say, Alright, in this particular rule, maybe the benefits justify the cost; in this other particular rule, same thing. But each one of those has costs that are added to the industry, and it's just going to start to take effect over time.

Back to the provision of liquidity. The cumulative effect of a lot of the costs of regulation has pushed out the bank dealers and brokers dealers, operating in a low interest rate environment, where the benefits are already low. Now we've added a bunch of new costs, so then they just say they're going to pull back. And early on, a lot of the regulators, particularly in the executive branch, or part of the administration, would say, No, no, it can't be Dodd-Frank. It can't be BASEL. It can't be these other things. We're finally starting to see a little bit of recognition from folks.[48] Maybe it is. Well, maybe it is. And so that's where conferences like this, empirical data, studies, all that sort of stuff, is really important to that conversation.

TABB: Questions for the commissioner?

Jim Toes: This isn't a political question. The commission right now comprises Chairman Mary Jo White, Commissioner Kara Stein, and you. We have two

---

[47] The Dodd-Frank Wall Street Reform and Consumer Protection Act is a massive piece of financial reform legislation passed during the Obama administration in 2010 as a response to the financial crisis of 2008. Named after sponsors Sen. Christopher J. Dodd (D-Conn.) and Rep. Barney Frank (D-Mass.), the act contains numerous provisions, spelled out over roughly 2300 pages, that were to be implemented over a period of several years.

Dodd-Frank established a number of new government agencies tasked with overseeing the various components of the act and, by extension, various aspects of the financial system. President Donald Trump pledged to repeal Dodd-Frank and, in May 2018, signed a new law rolling back significant portions of it. Source: Investopedia.

[48] See Basel Accords, www.investopedia.com/terms/b/basel_accord.asp
Source: Investopedia.

additional commissioners, for a total of five, who obviously didn't get approved. And now there is the election coming up.[49] What happens if these two are not approved by the Senate by the end of the year? Under that scenario, where the two are nominated and pass the committee stage but still fall short of final approval by January 1st, how does the SEC then look?[50]

PIWOWAR: For those of you not familiar with this, the SEC normally has five commissioners. By statute, the president can only name three from his own party. Two have to come from the other party. If you haven't guessed by now, I'm a Republican commissioner, so I'm not a big fan of a lot of the Dodd-Frank stuff. We are currently down to three commissioners because a couple of terms have ended. Two have been nominated by the President, and they've gone through the Senate and the committee.

They're on the floor right now, and they haven't gone forward. And so, unfortunately, it becomes sort of a political fight over a political issue, and political spending disclosure. It has nothing to do with the qualifications of either of the nominees. They're both highly qualified. I know one of them very well. I've gotten to know the other one very well too. I would love to see them there sooner rather than later. We have a lot of important work to get done.

The Commission works best when we're at full strength. It works best when we identify discretionary issues we think need to be tackled by having conversations with industry members, instead of dealing with highly politicized issues like Dodd-Frank. I'm hopeful that those two Commission nominees still get through by the end of the next session. We'll have to see what happens after that. Then obviously, it depends, in terms of who is elected the next US president. How many days are we down to now? Is it seven? Seven and an hour from the US presidential election day! Somebody reminded me we have an extra hour because we turn our clocks back. Just when you thought it was over, you've got another hour of this stuff! And once we get past the election, the new SEC chair will be determined.

TABB: And, of course, there will be scandal involved with just that extra hour alone!

PIWOWAR: We do have a lot of work still to get done in the meantime. I think some of it we can get done in the sort of lame-duck period. We have a deadline coming up on the Consolidated Audit Trail, to finalize the order on that.[51]

TABB: Do we think that will actually get voted on?

[49] With SEC head's resignation, field clears for Trump to cut back regulations—The Washington Post. www.washingtonpost.com/business/economy/2016/11/14/b1dc4058-a91a-11e6-8fc0-7be8f848c492_story.html

[50] See SEC Historical Summary of Chairmen and Commissioners. https://www.sec.gov/about/sechistoricalsummary.htm

Source: Securities and Exchange Commission.

[51] See the Consolidated Audit Plan (CATS) https://www.catnmsplan.com/index.html

PIWOWAR: We're going to do that and put it out there finally. It's a multiyear process. But you think back, what precipitated that was the Flash Crash of 2010.[52] Ian Domowitz pointed out on the last panel that it took us a year to sort of get that study published.[53] The reason why is because it took us so long to collect all the data from all the disparate data sources. It will be nice that we finally get the Consolidated Audit Trail up and running. But we've only got one shot to get this thing right, so we want to make sure we get everything right.

And the CAT, I think, will be very helpful in terms of our ability to monitor the markets and protect investors and make sure the markets remain fair and efficient.

BILL HART [Modern Markets Initiative]: How closely are you paying attention to the debate over CFTC's Reg AT and the changes that it would make?[54]

PIWOWAR: Not as much as other stuff. I mean this is the one on the concern about information.

TABB: About access to algorithms?

PIWOWAR: Yes, right. I mean it's obviously outside of our jurisdiction. But I think there is a crossover. Here is a concern that I have. Folks ask me what keeps me up at night. It's cybersecurity issues. And it's not just cybersecurity issues related to our registrants. The public companies have to let their investors know if there is material information. It's not just our regulated entities, but it's the governments, the regulators, our access to proprietary algorithms, to personally identifiable information, or PII. There is going to be a lot of PII in the Consolidated Audit Trail—and these are things that I worry about.[55] It's like what should the regulator be getting? And if it's appropriate for the regulator to be getting that information, what sort of protections do we need to make sure that we have it locked down so that this information doesn't get into the wrong hands?

TABB: Commissioner Piwowar, on that sober note, thank you very much. We very much appreciate you being here.

PIWOWAR: My pleasure. Thank you.

---

[52] The Flash Crash of May 6, 2010, lasted about 36 minutes, erasing 998.5 points or about 9% in the Dow Jones Industrial Average and then quickly recouping the losses as the various indexes rapidly rebounded in this high-speed, electronic trading phenomena. At the time, it was a record one-day point decline on an intraday basis in the history of Dow Jones Industrial Average.

[53] See Chap. 5. New Approaches for Creating Liquidity.

[54] CFTC Withdraws Reg AT and Approves Electronic Trading Proposal in June 2020 Meeting—Eventus Systems

www.eventussystems.com/cftc-withdraws-reg-at-and-approves-electronic-trading-proposal-in-june-2020-meeting/#:~

Source: Eventus Systems.

[55] The Consolidated Audit Trail and Customer PII: Why take the risk—The Consolidated Audit Trail and Customer PII: Why take the risk—SIFMA.

www.sifma.org/resources/news/the-consolidated-audit-trail-and-customer-pii-why-take-the-ris
Source: SIFMA.

FSC
www.fsc.org
MIX
Papier aus verantwortungsvollen Quellen
Paper from responsible sources
FSC® C105338

If you have any concerns about our products,
you can contact us on
ProductSafety@springernature.com

In case Publisher is established outside the EU,
the EU authorized representative is:
Springer Nature Customer Service Center GmbH
Europaplatz 3, 69115 Heidelberg, Germany

Printed by Libri Plureos GmbH
in Hamburg, Germany